LARGE PRINT

COLORING BOOK

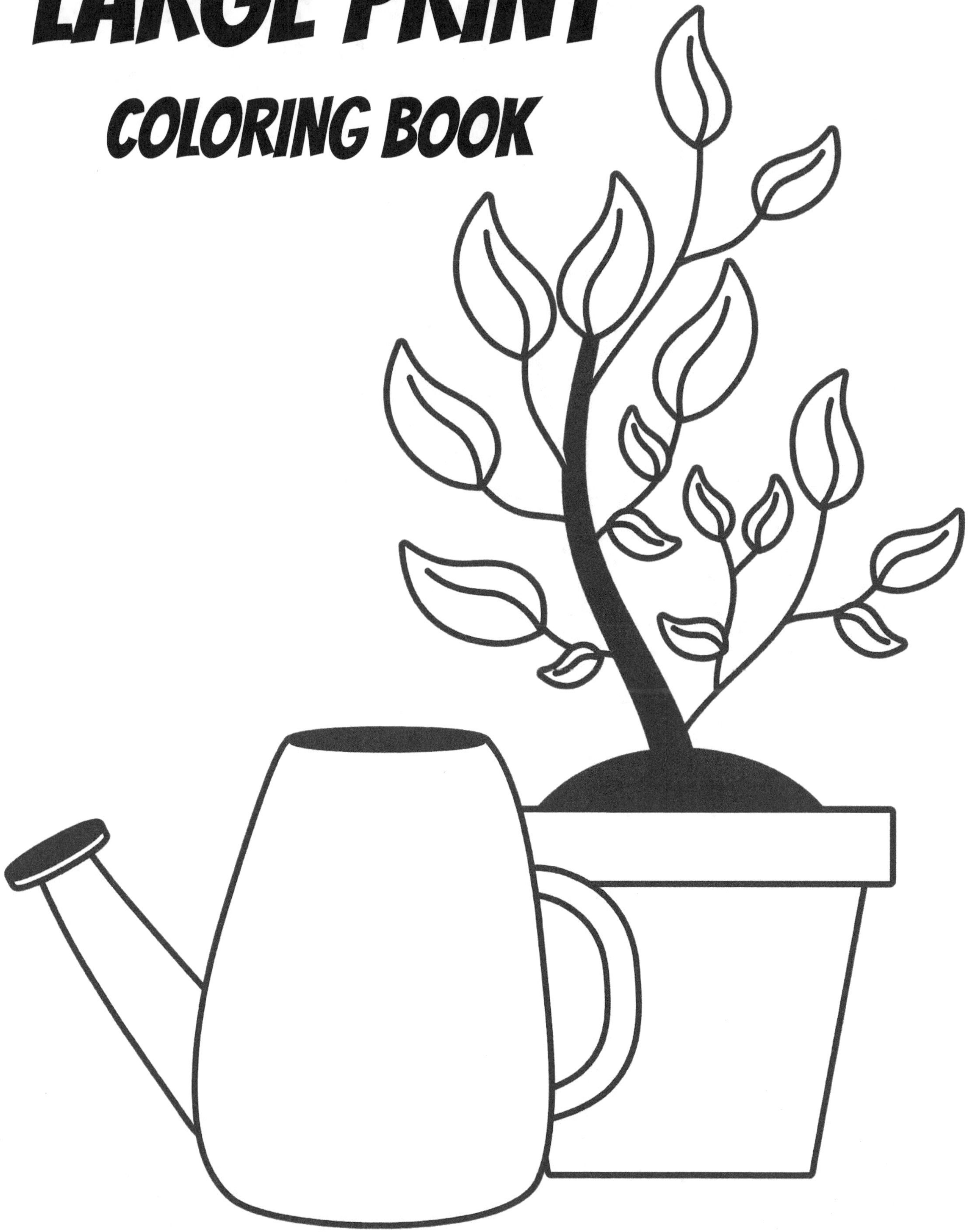

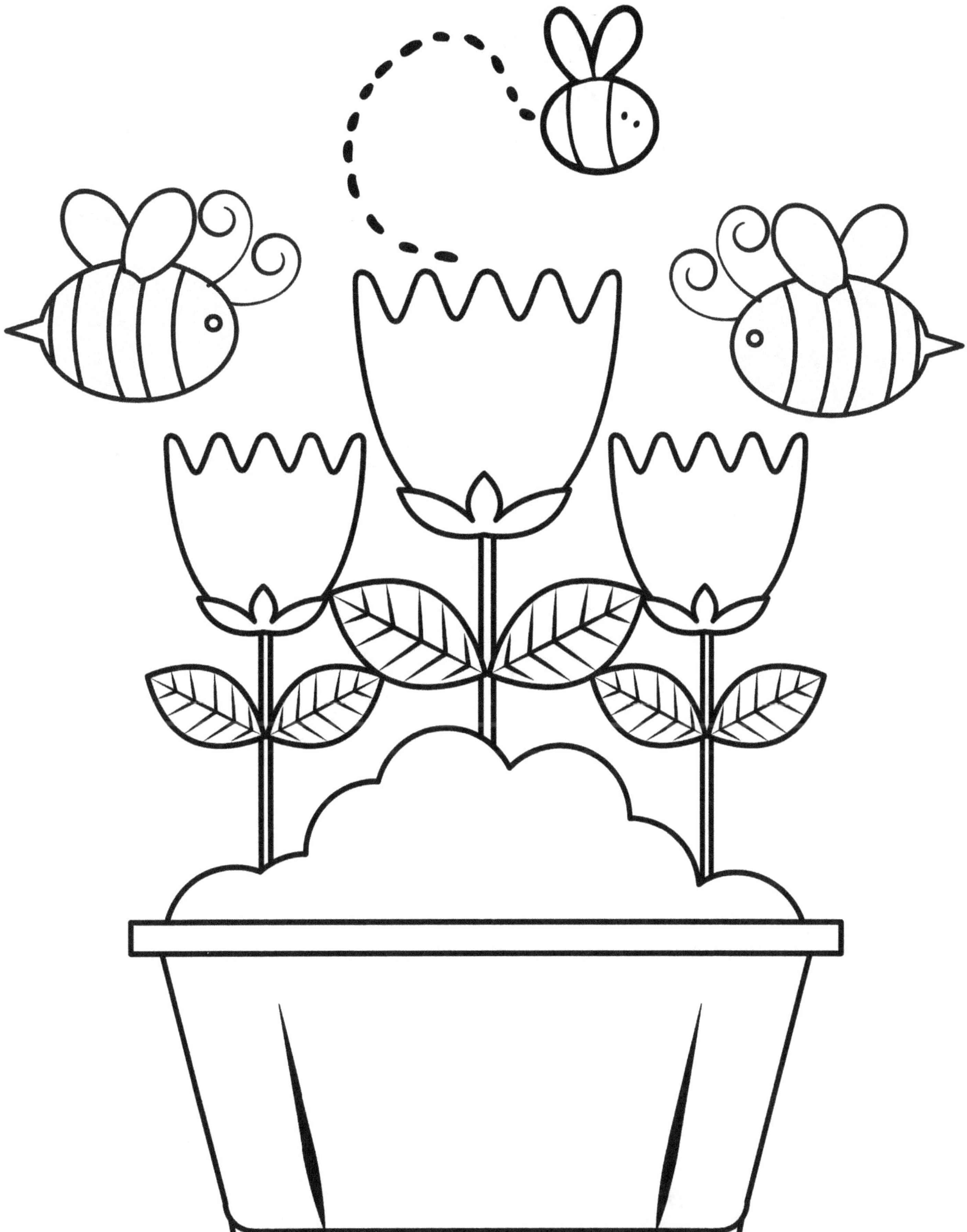

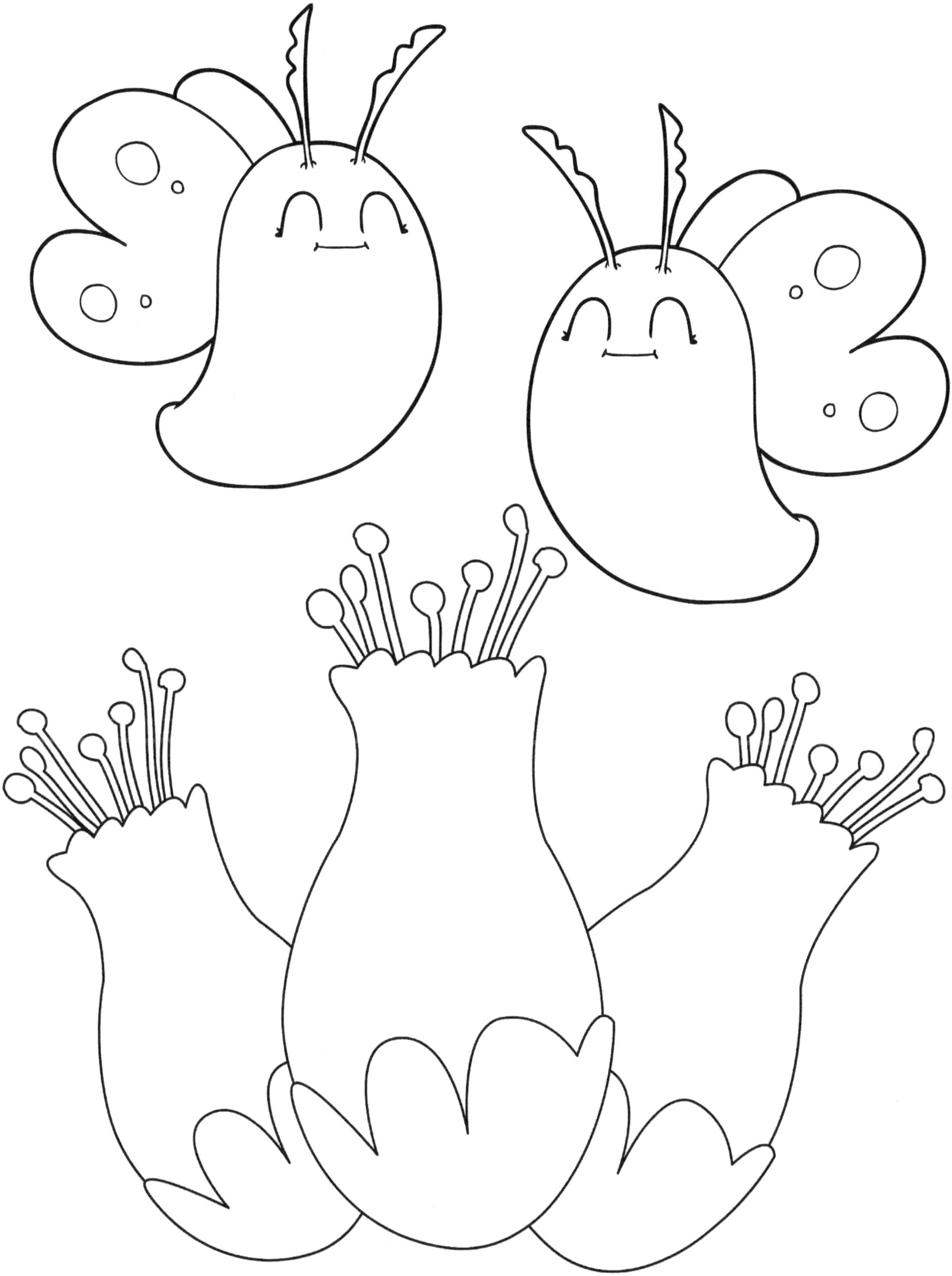

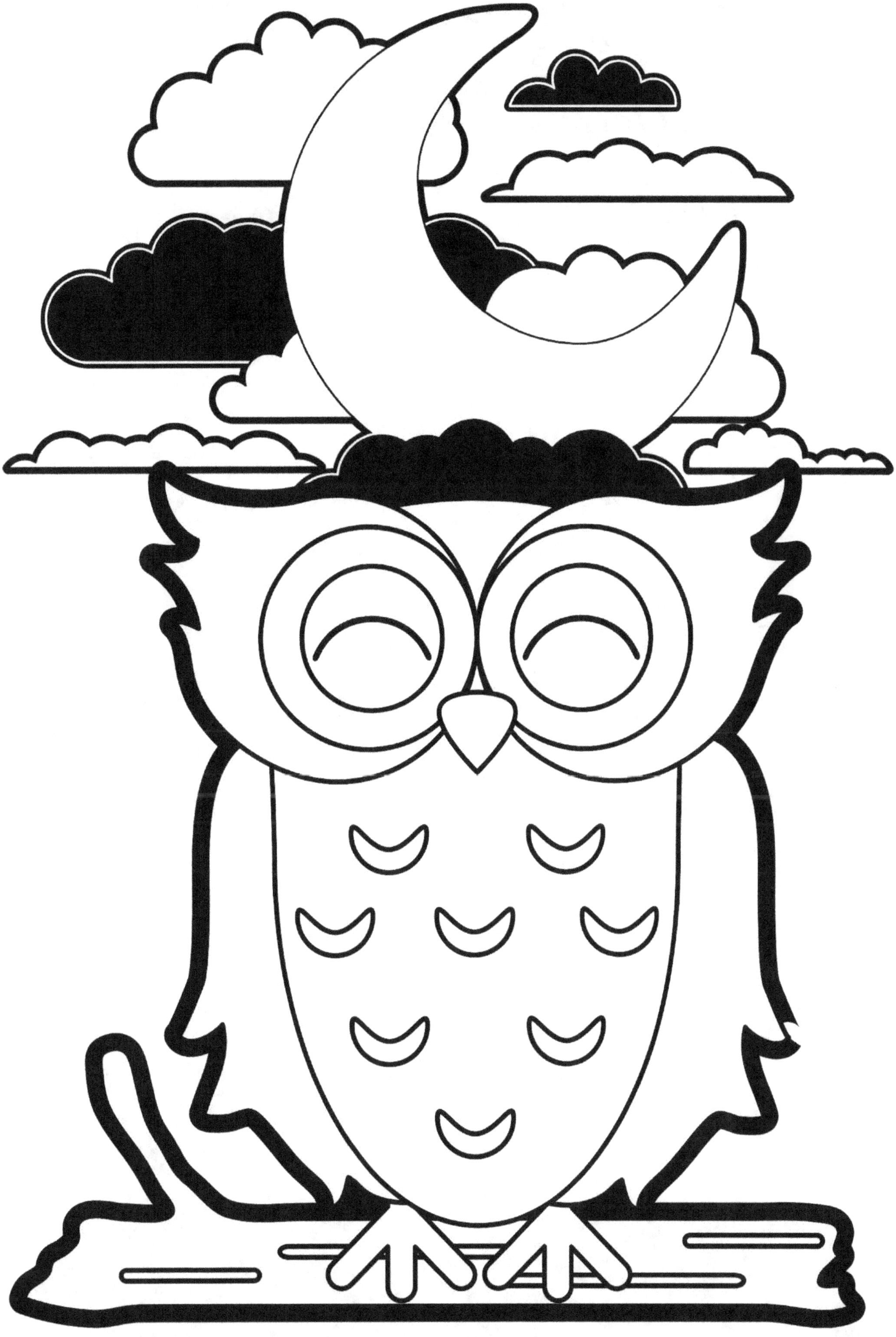

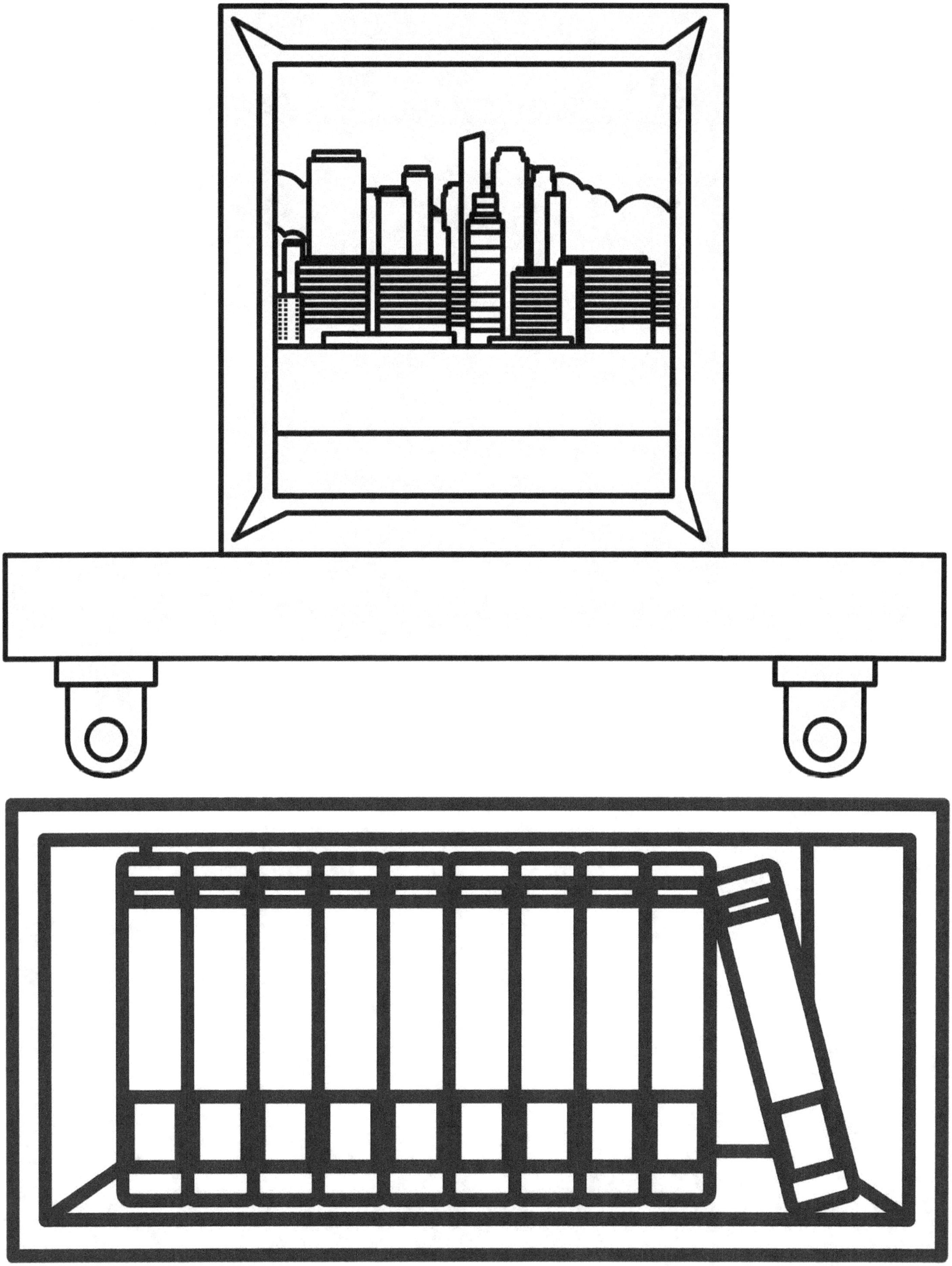

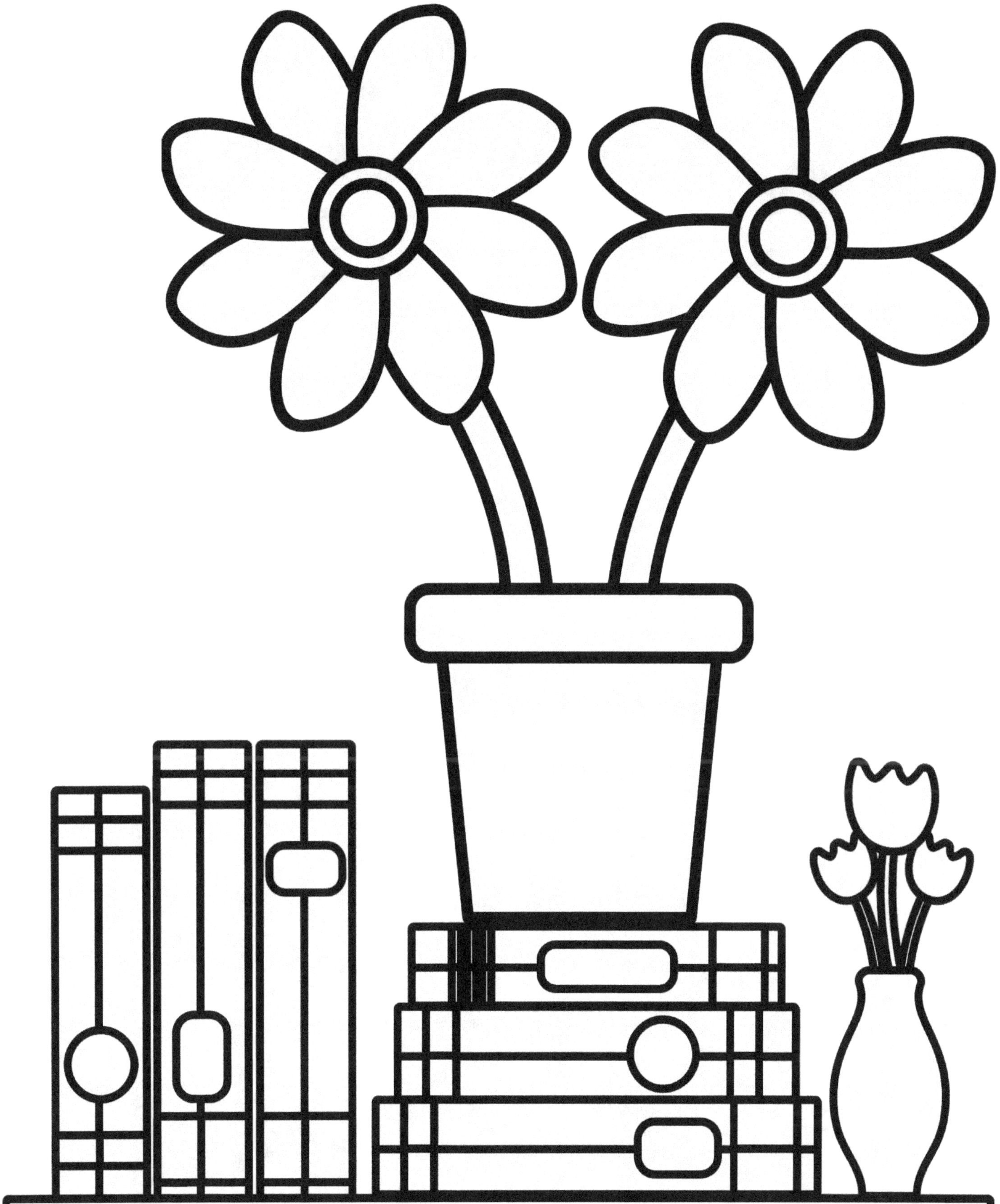

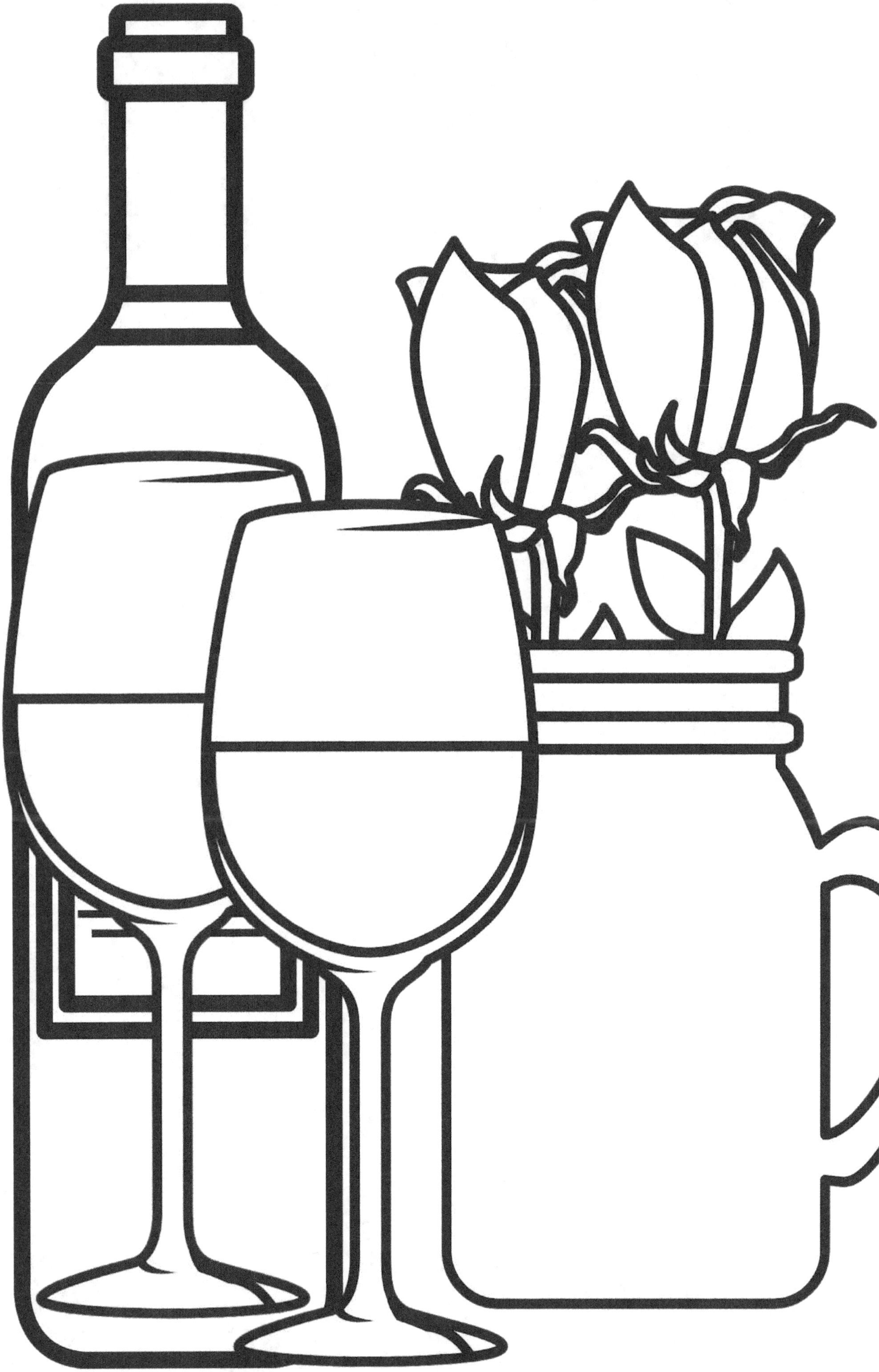

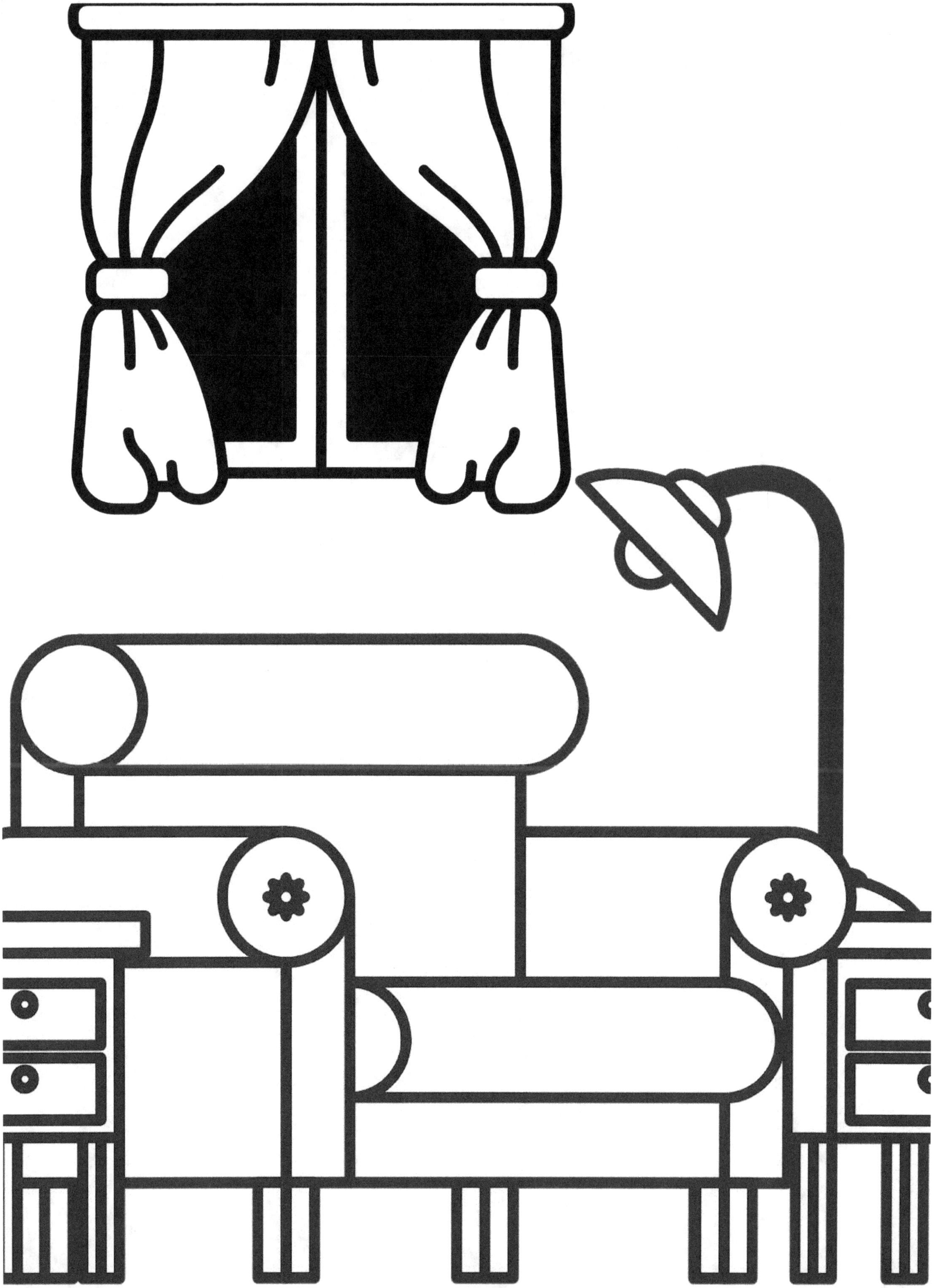

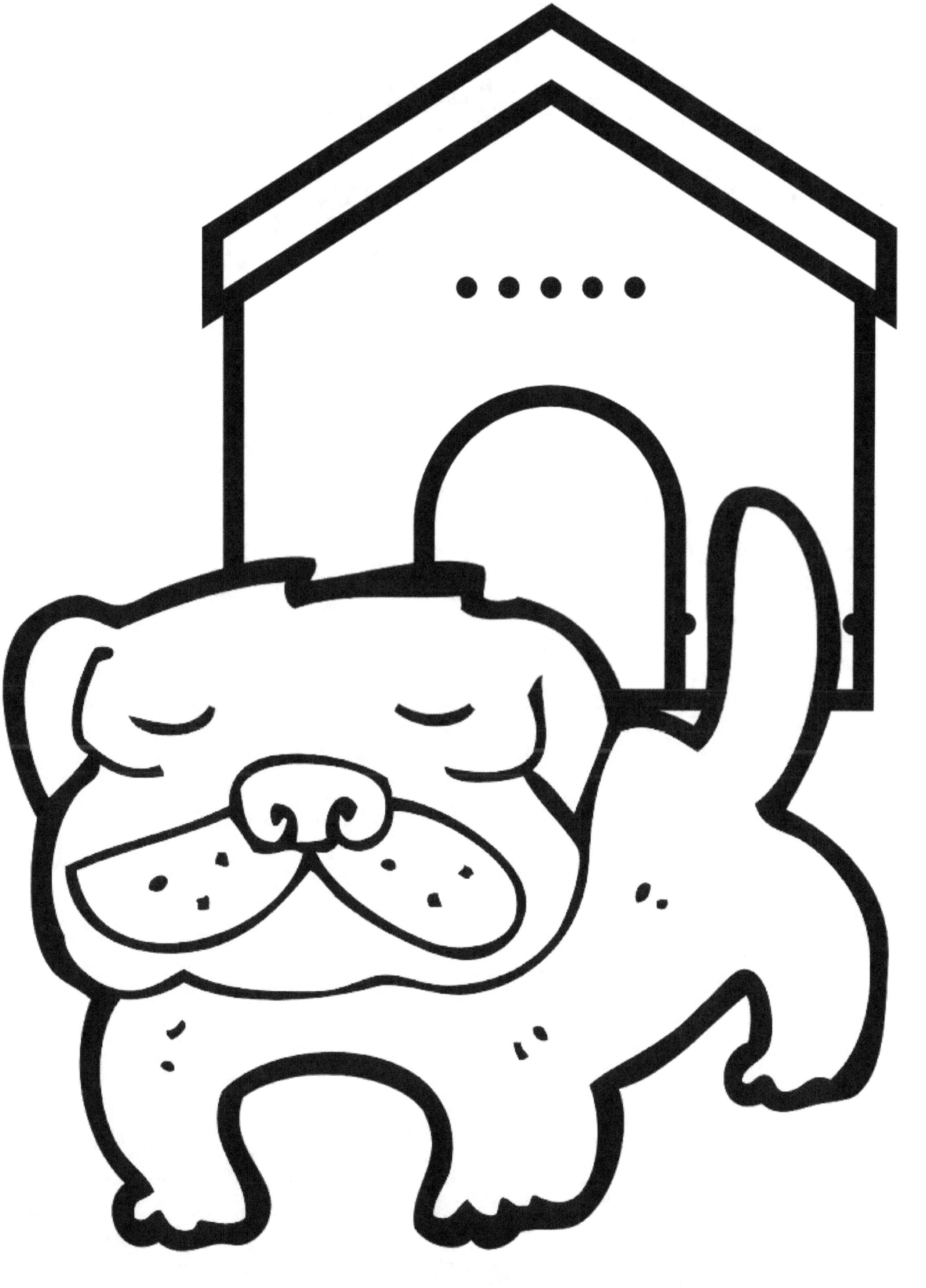

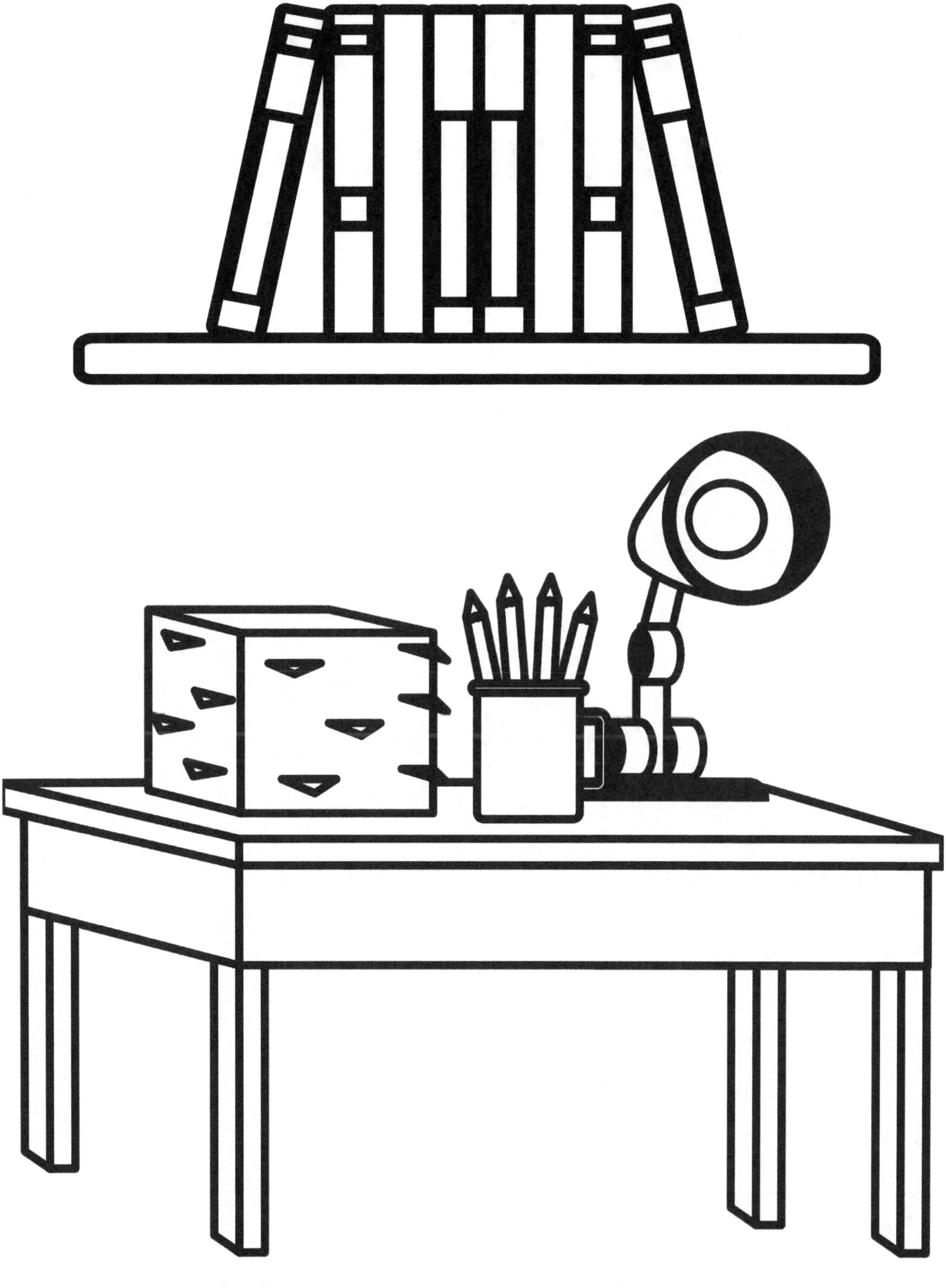

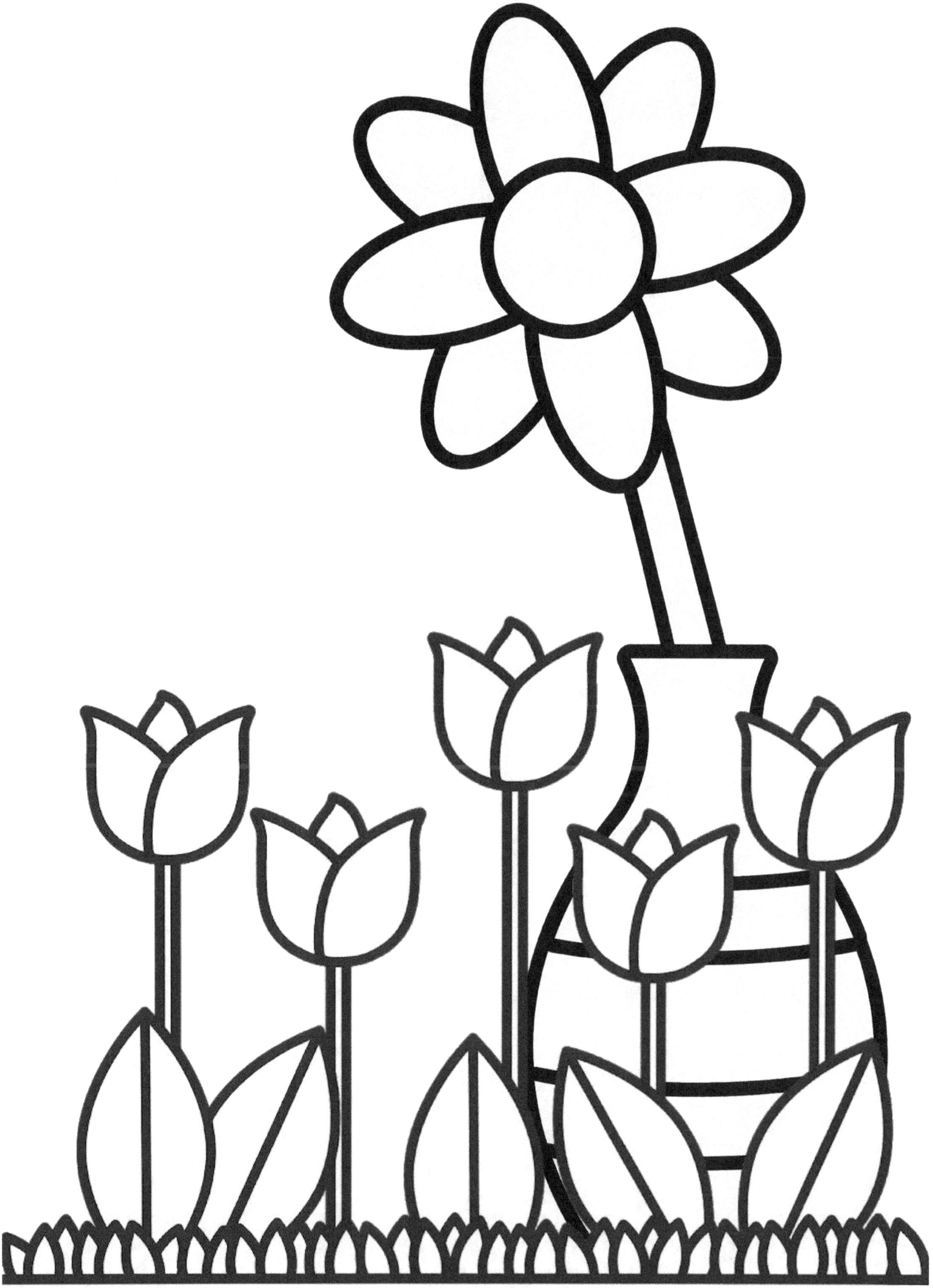

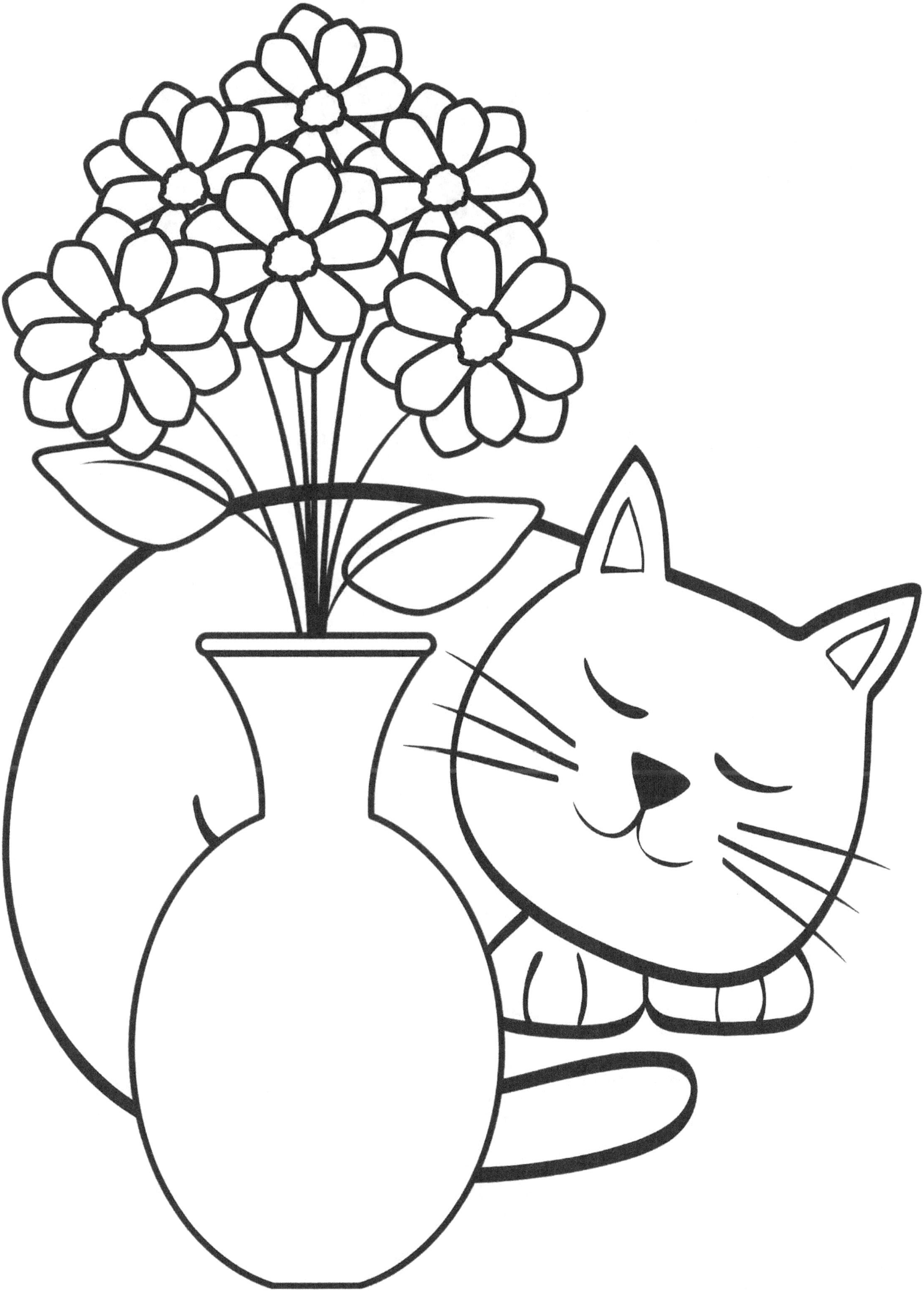

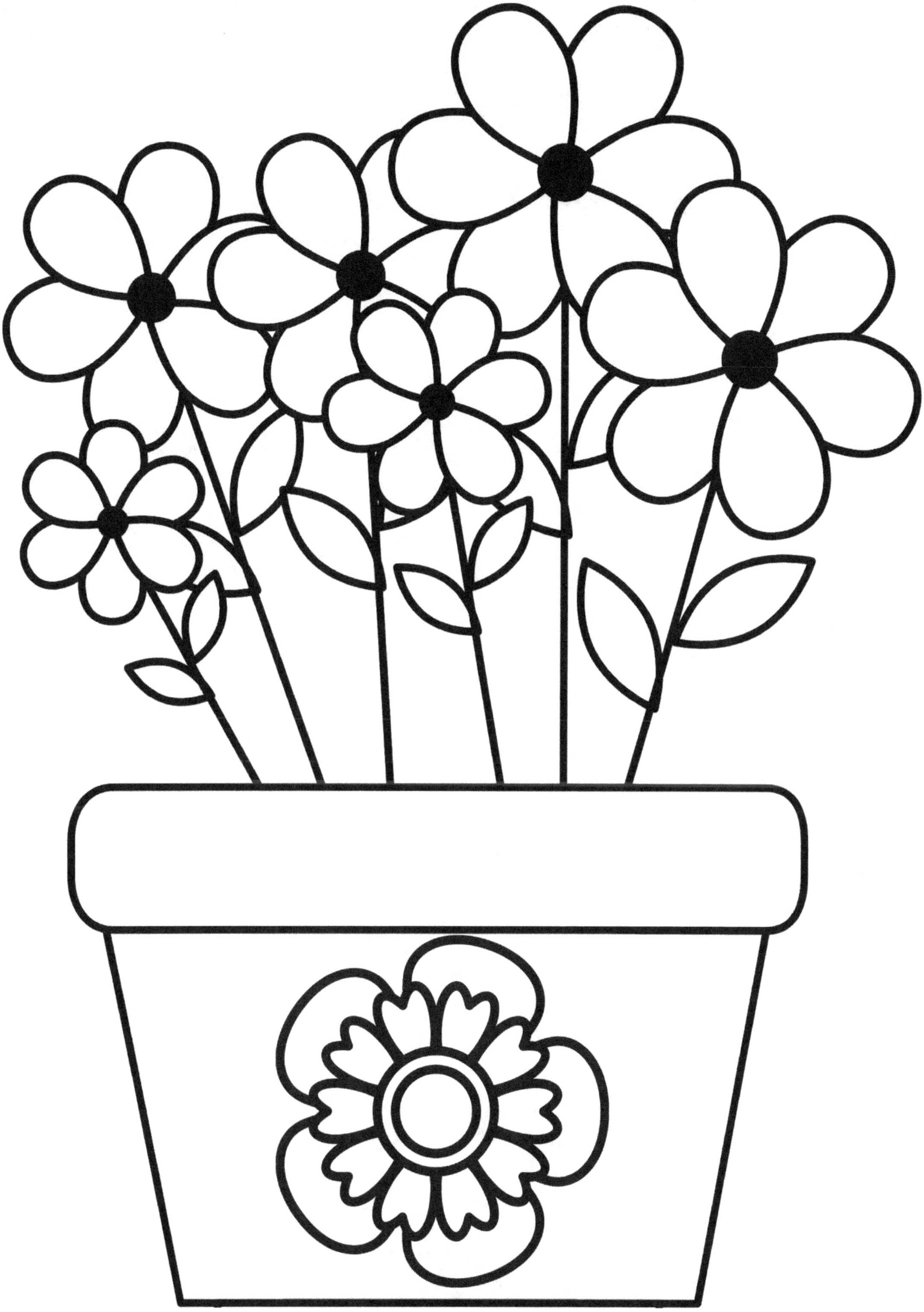

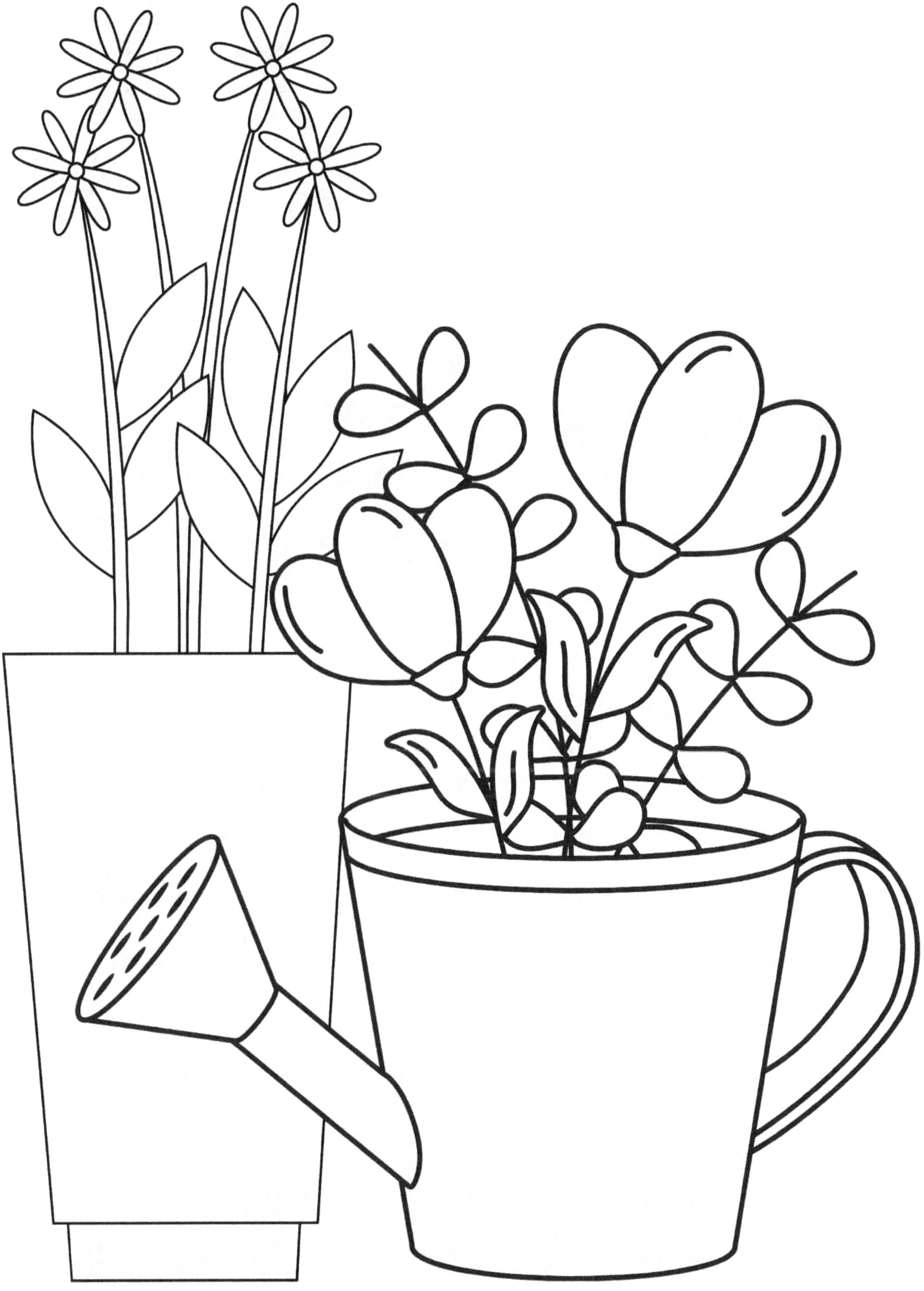

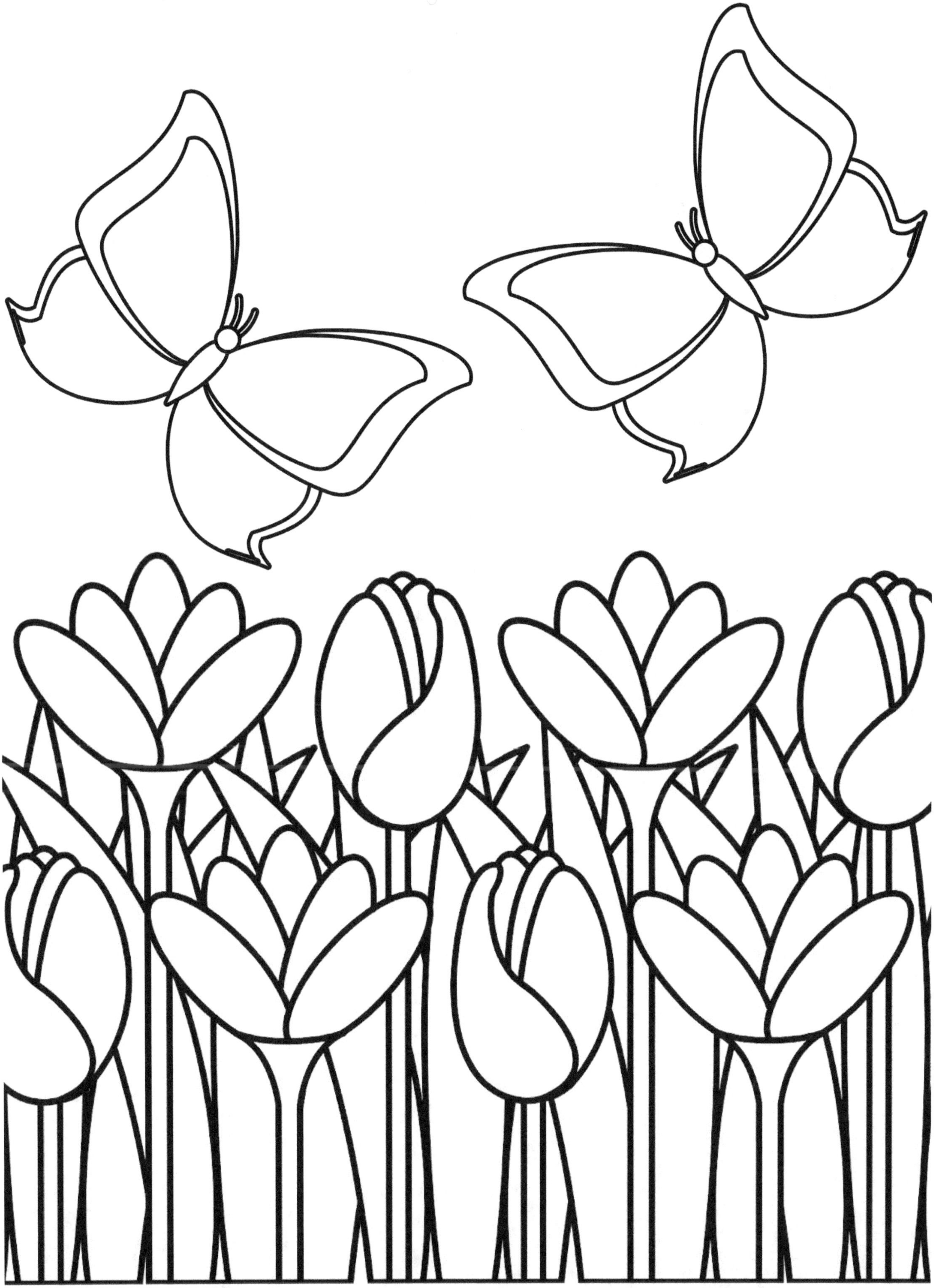

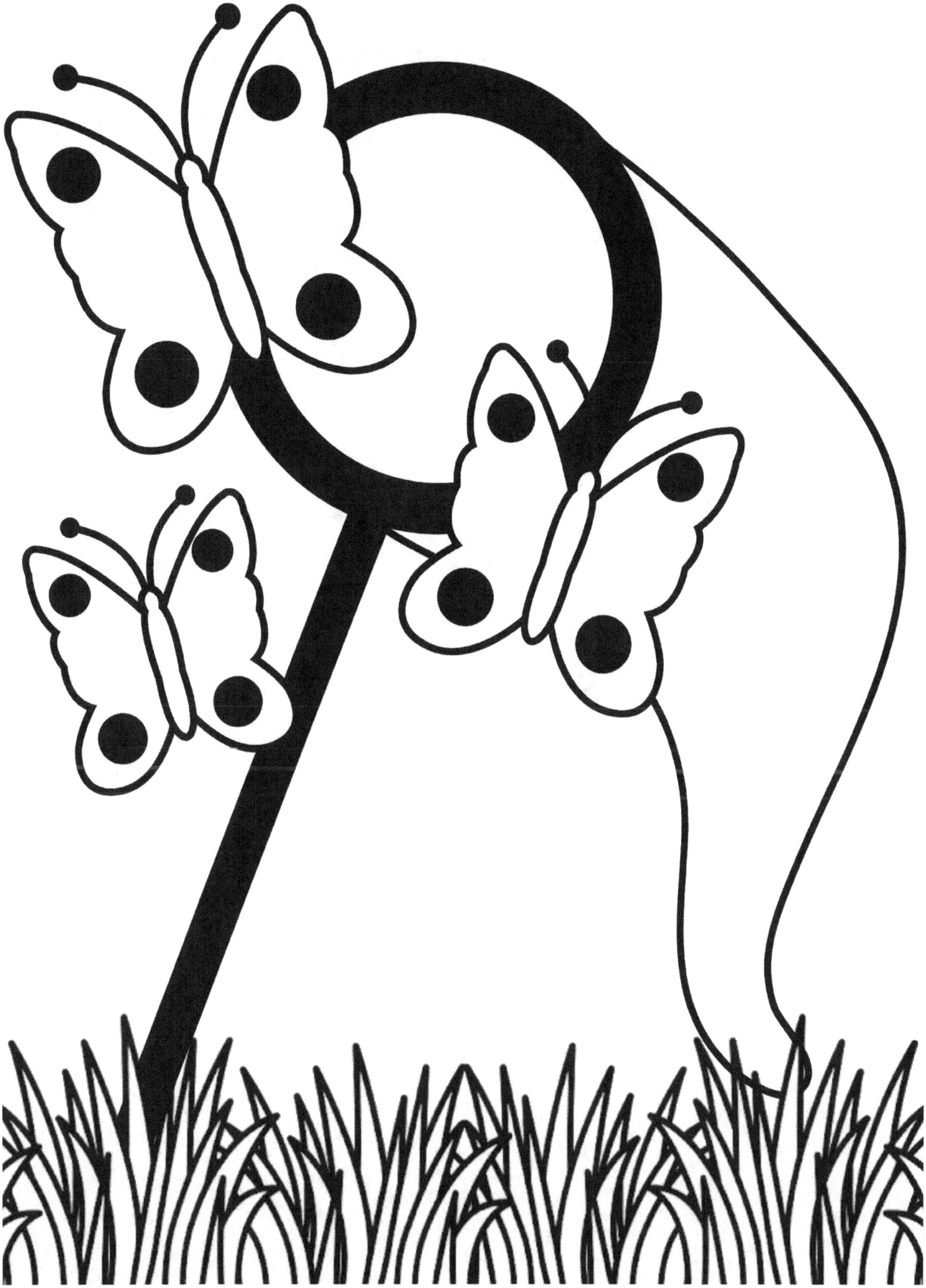

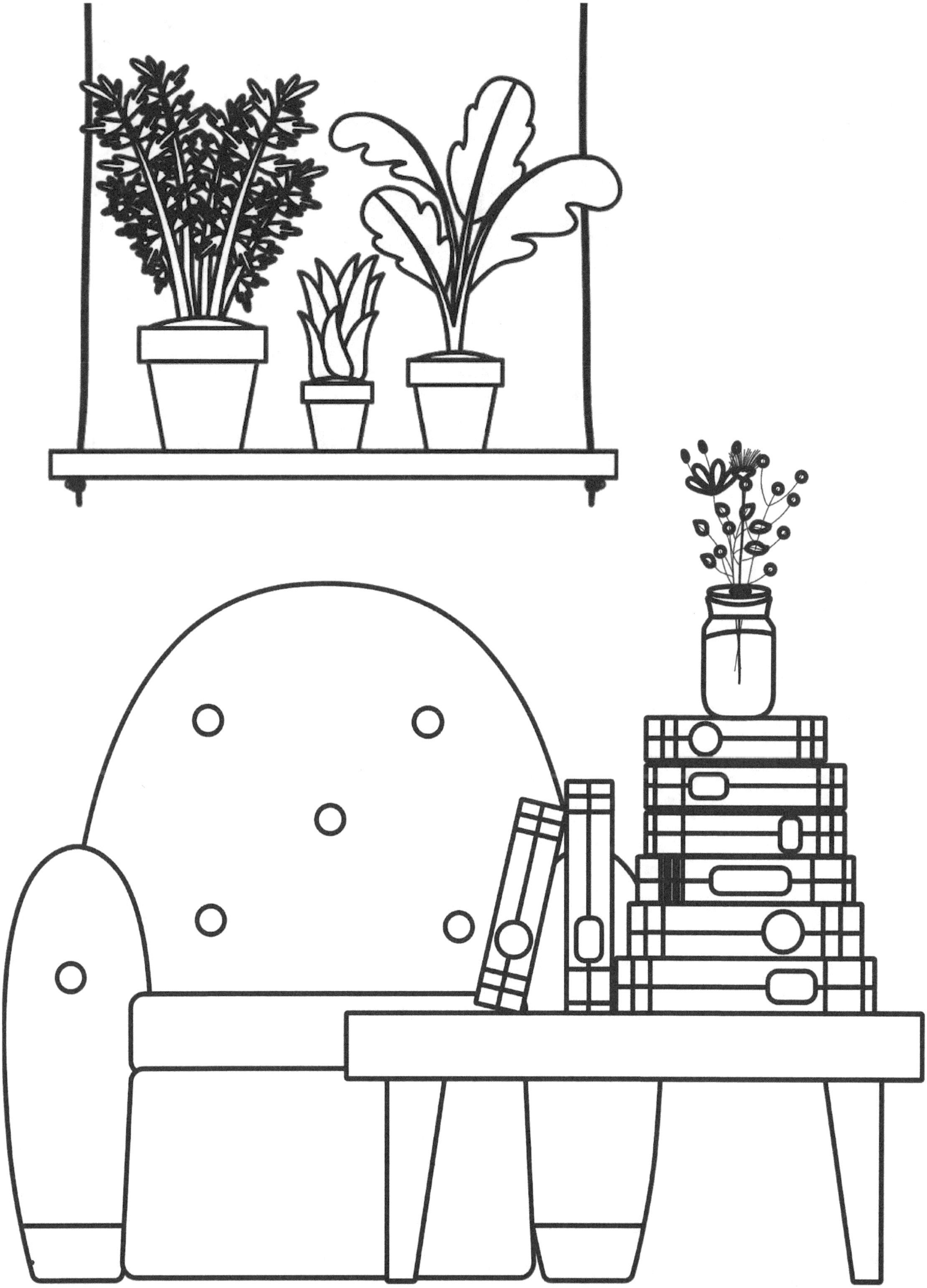

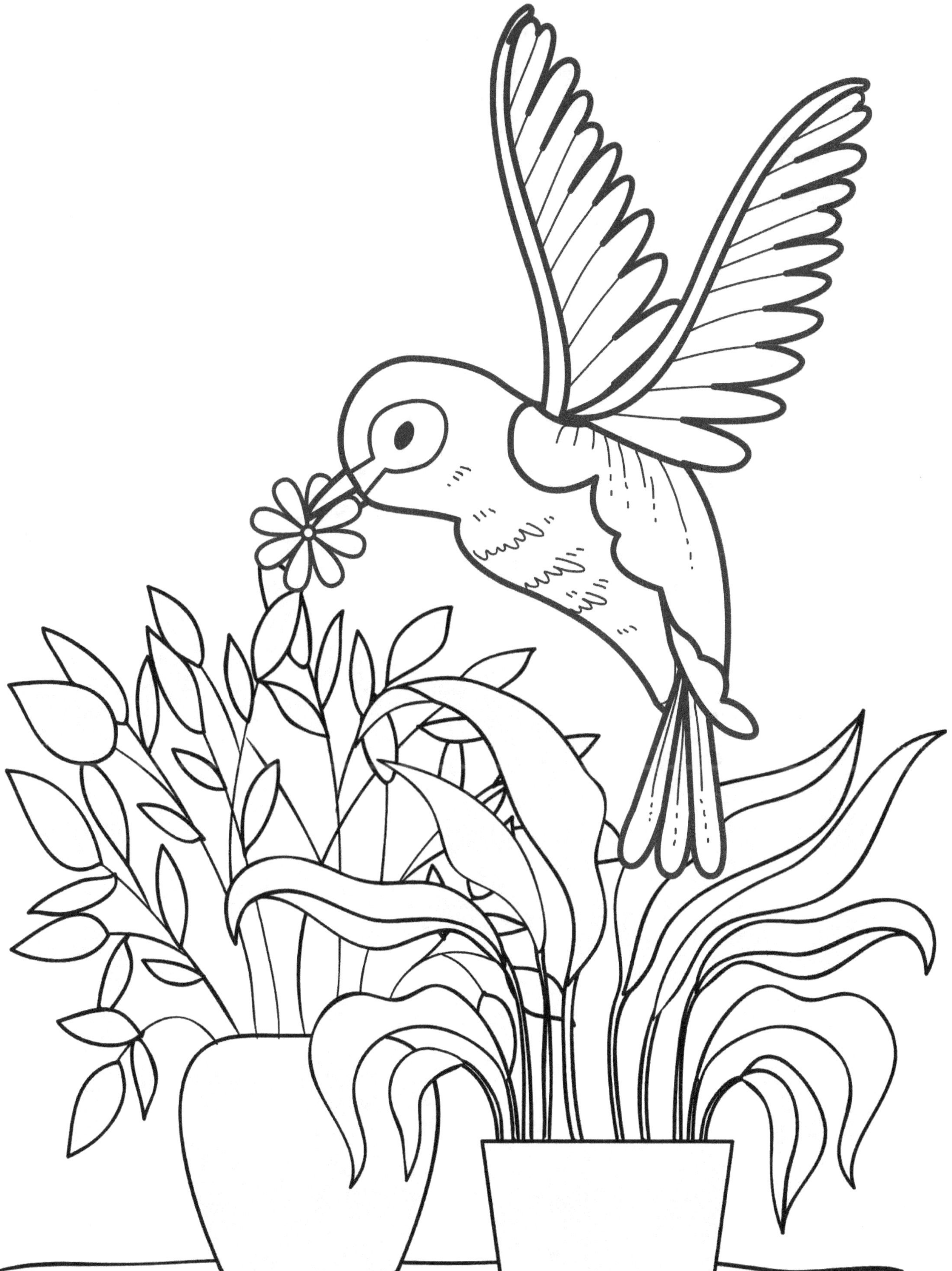

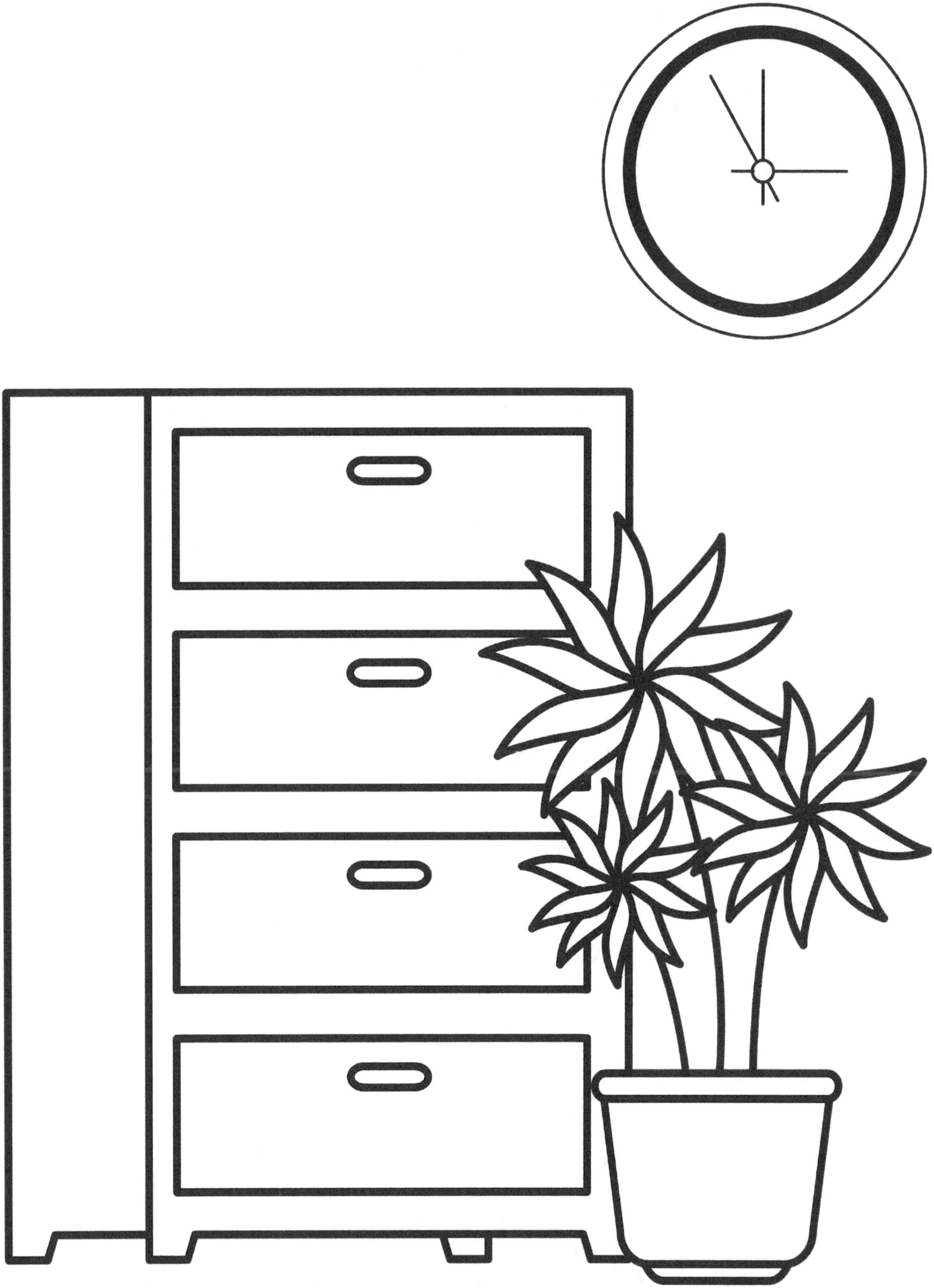

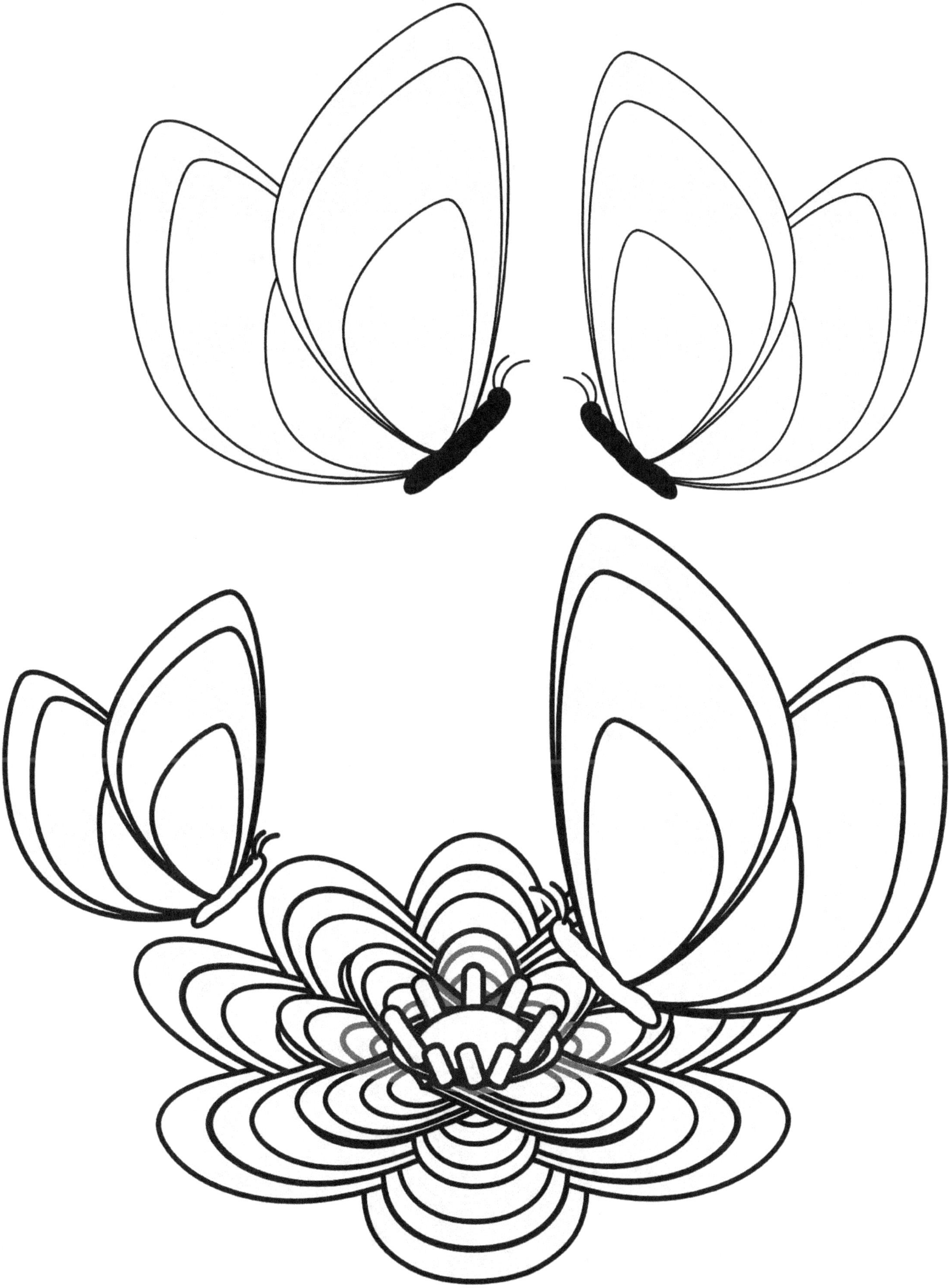

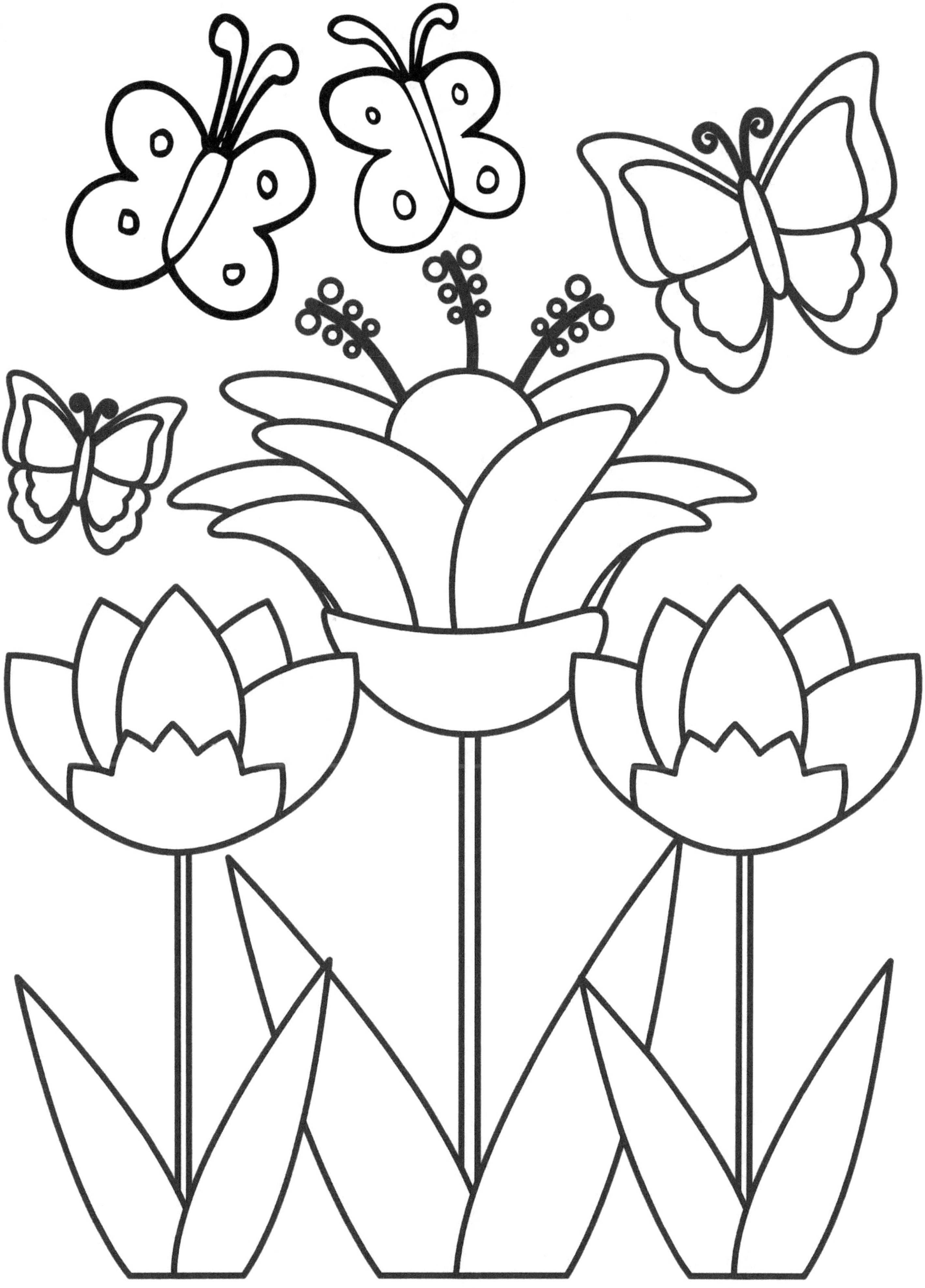

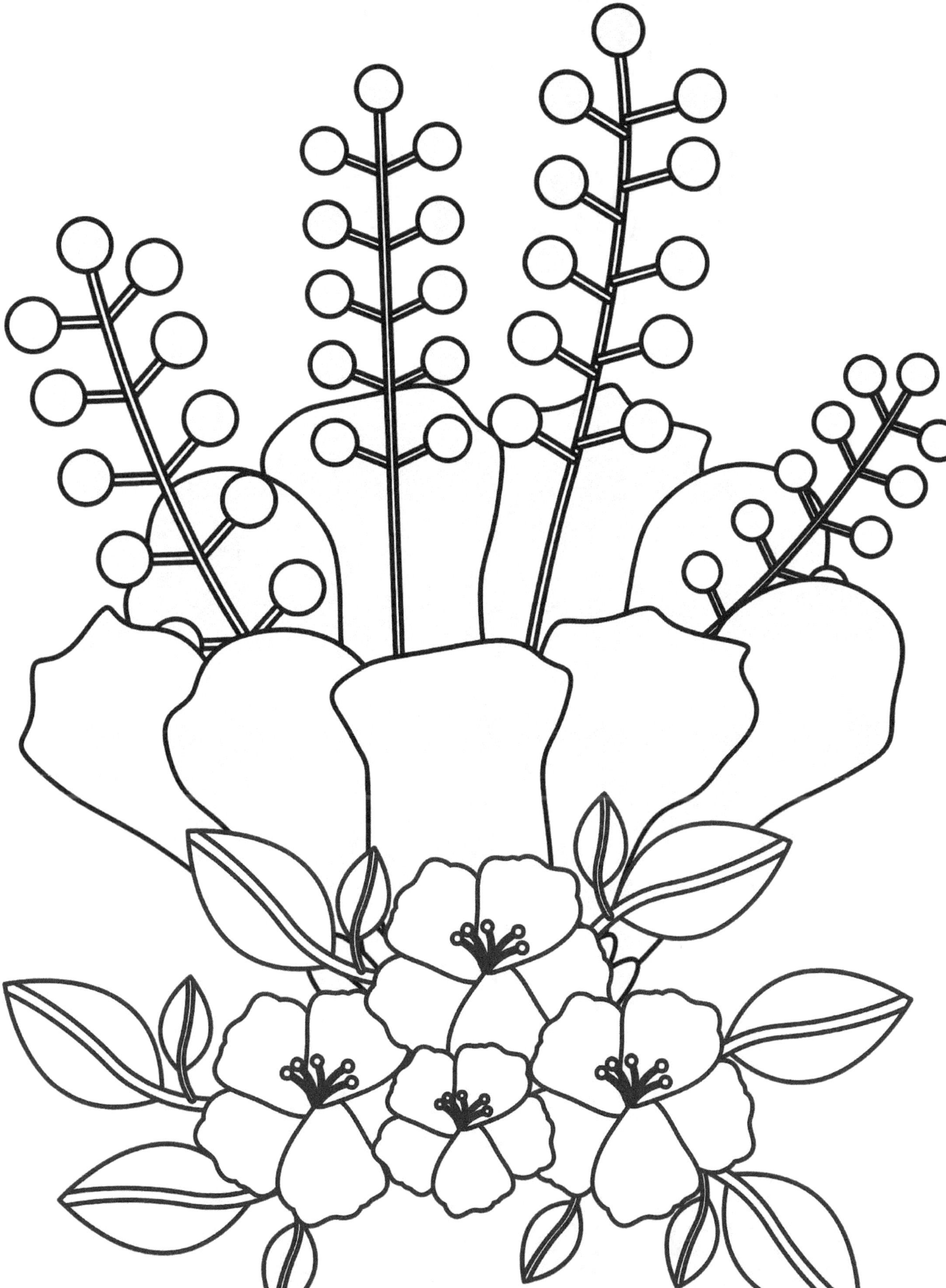

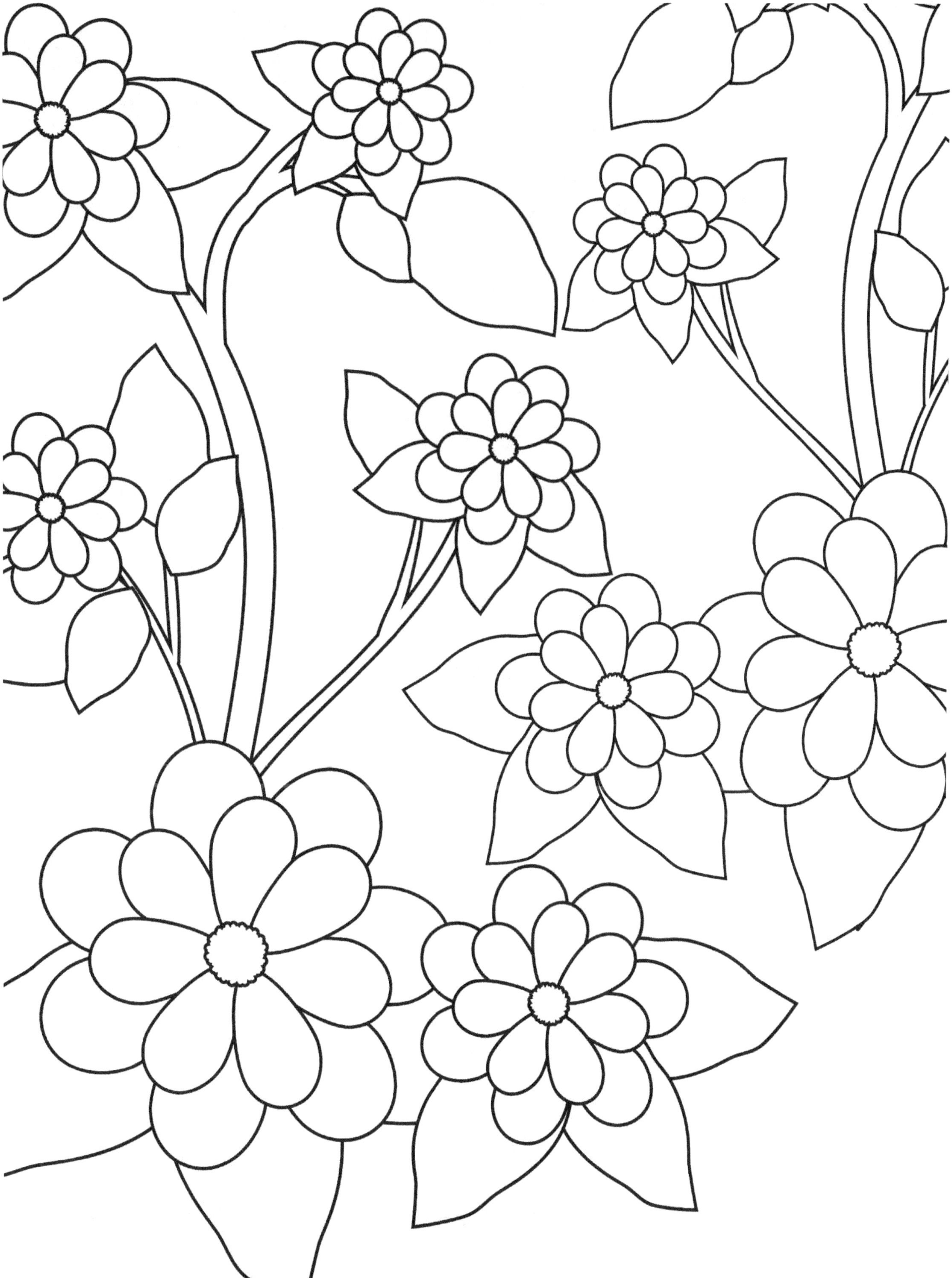

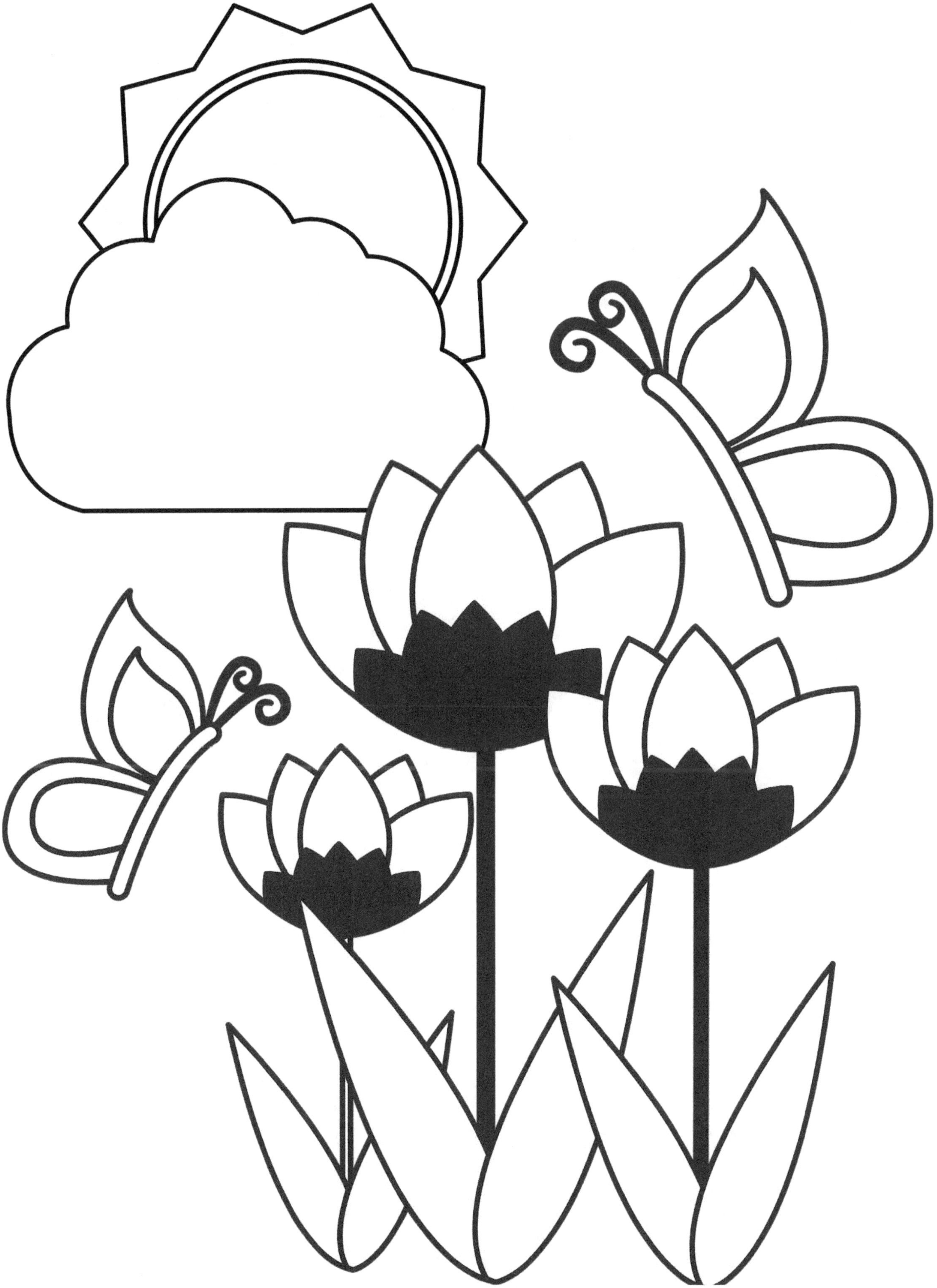

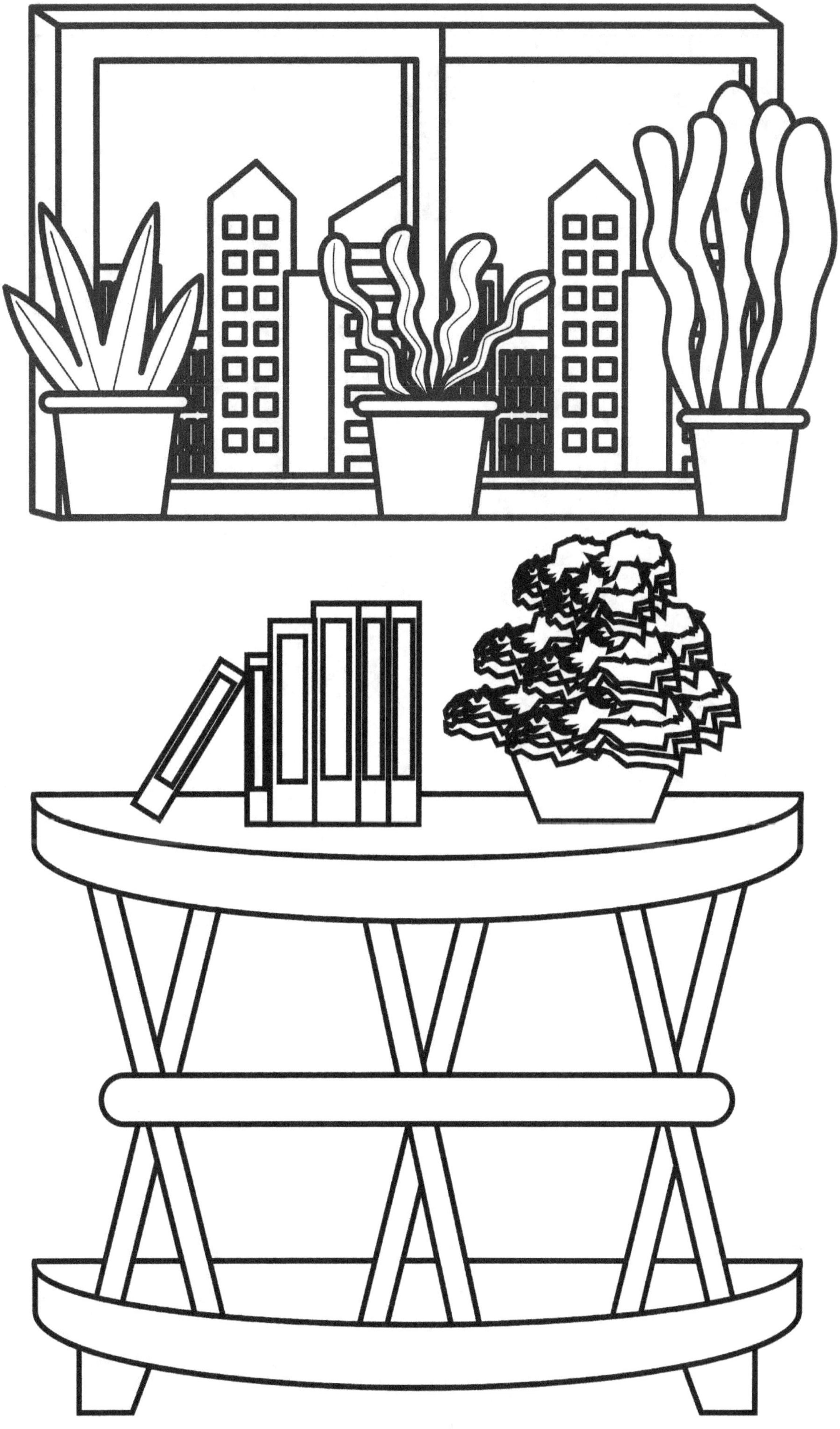

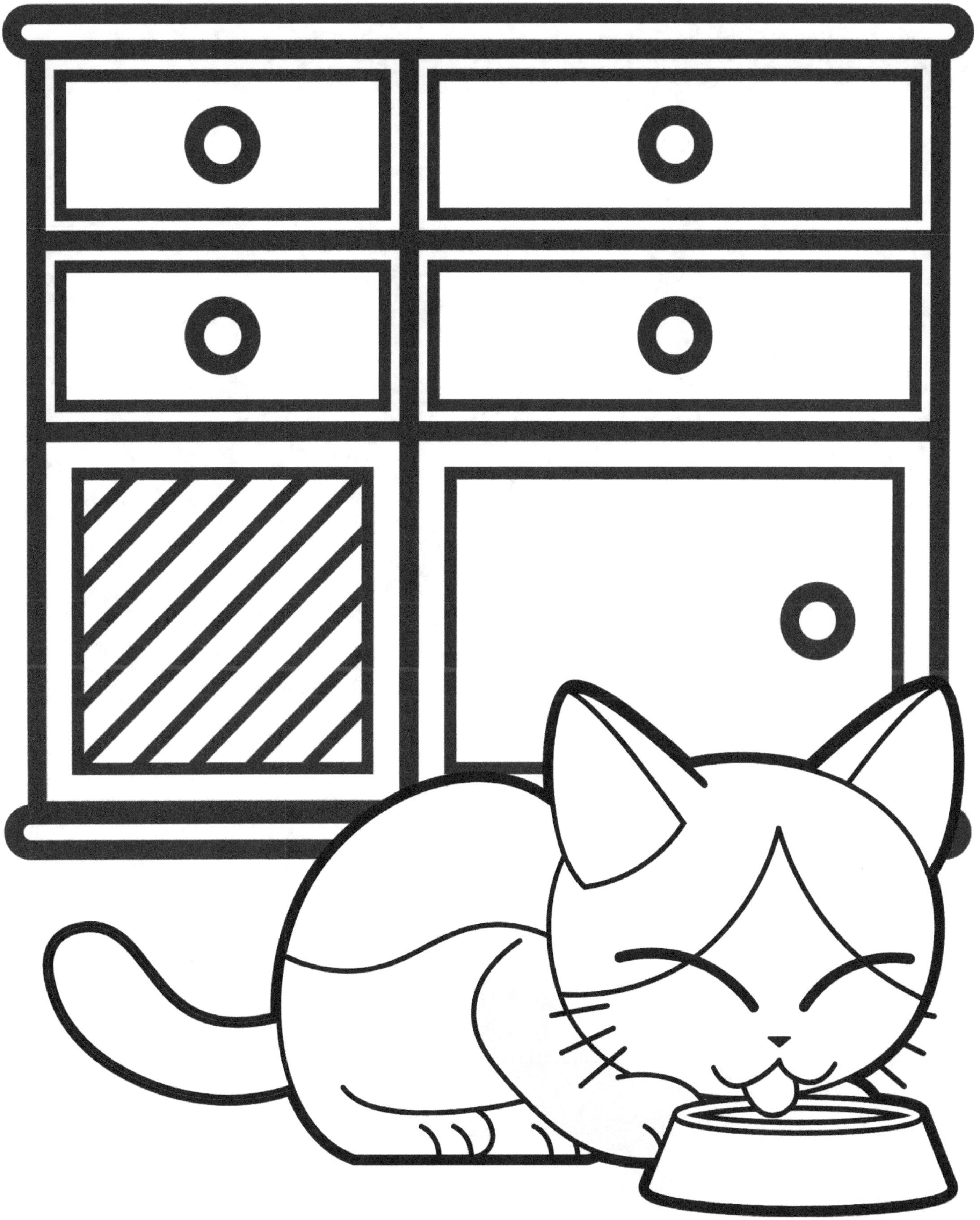

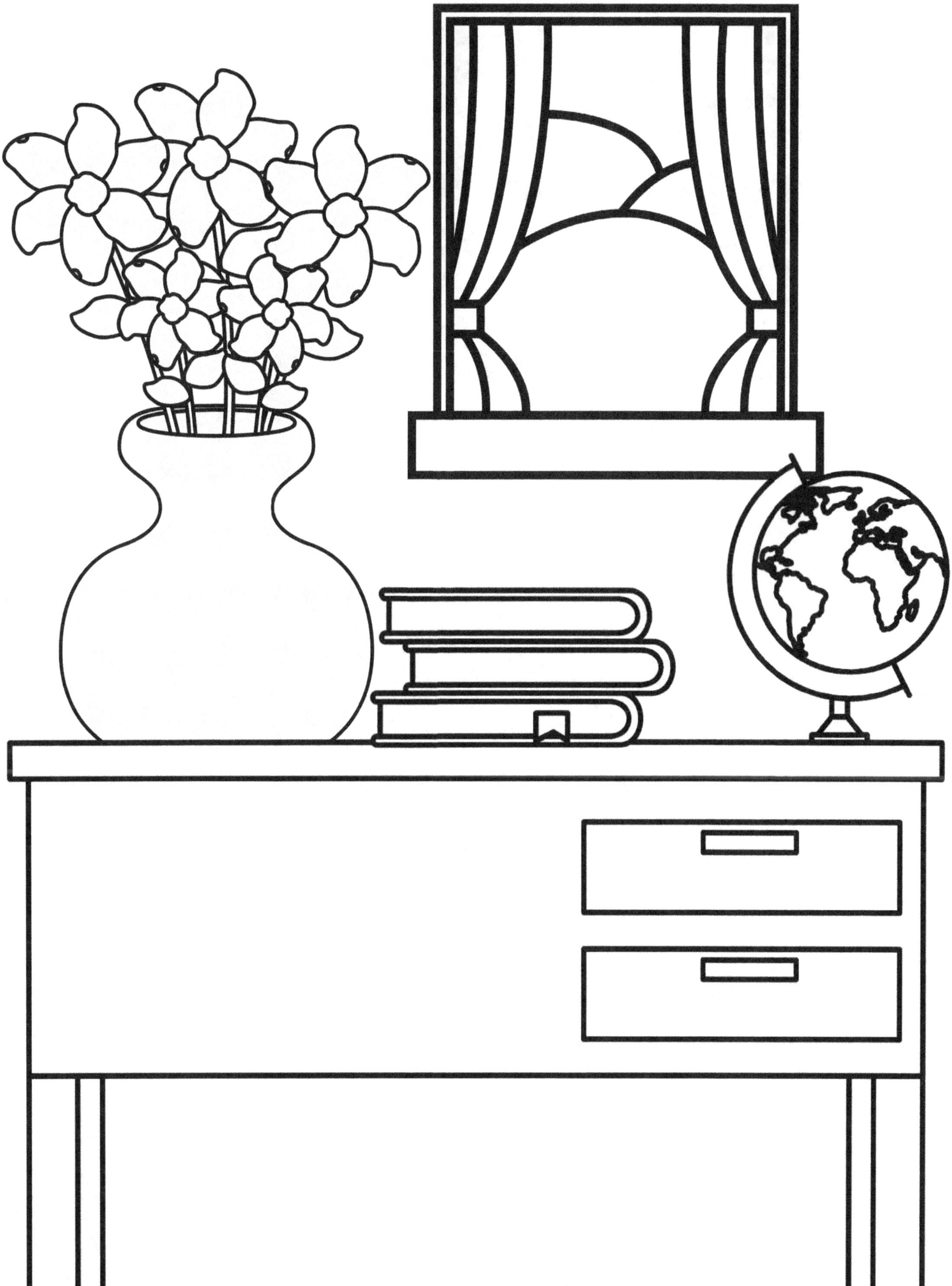

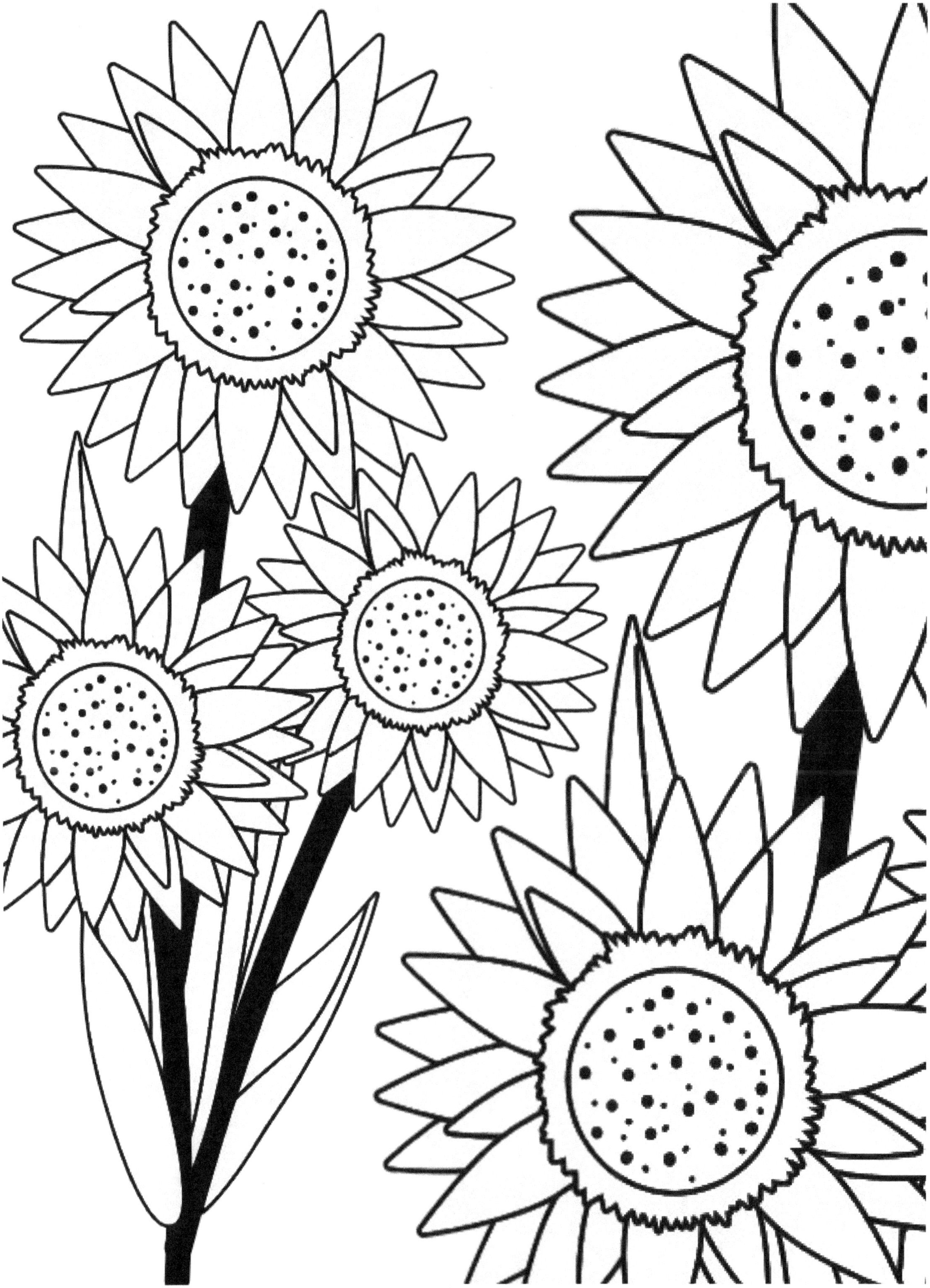

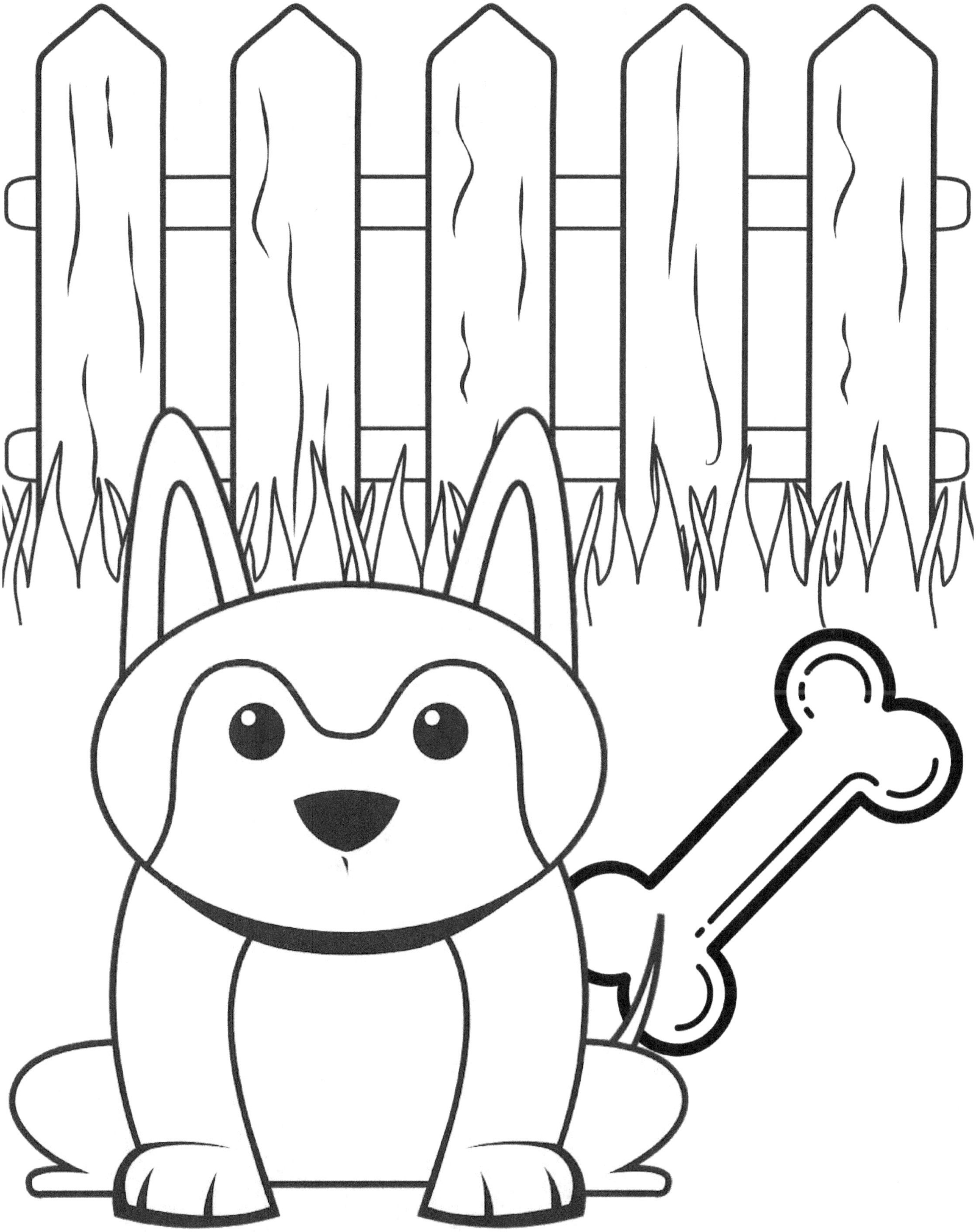

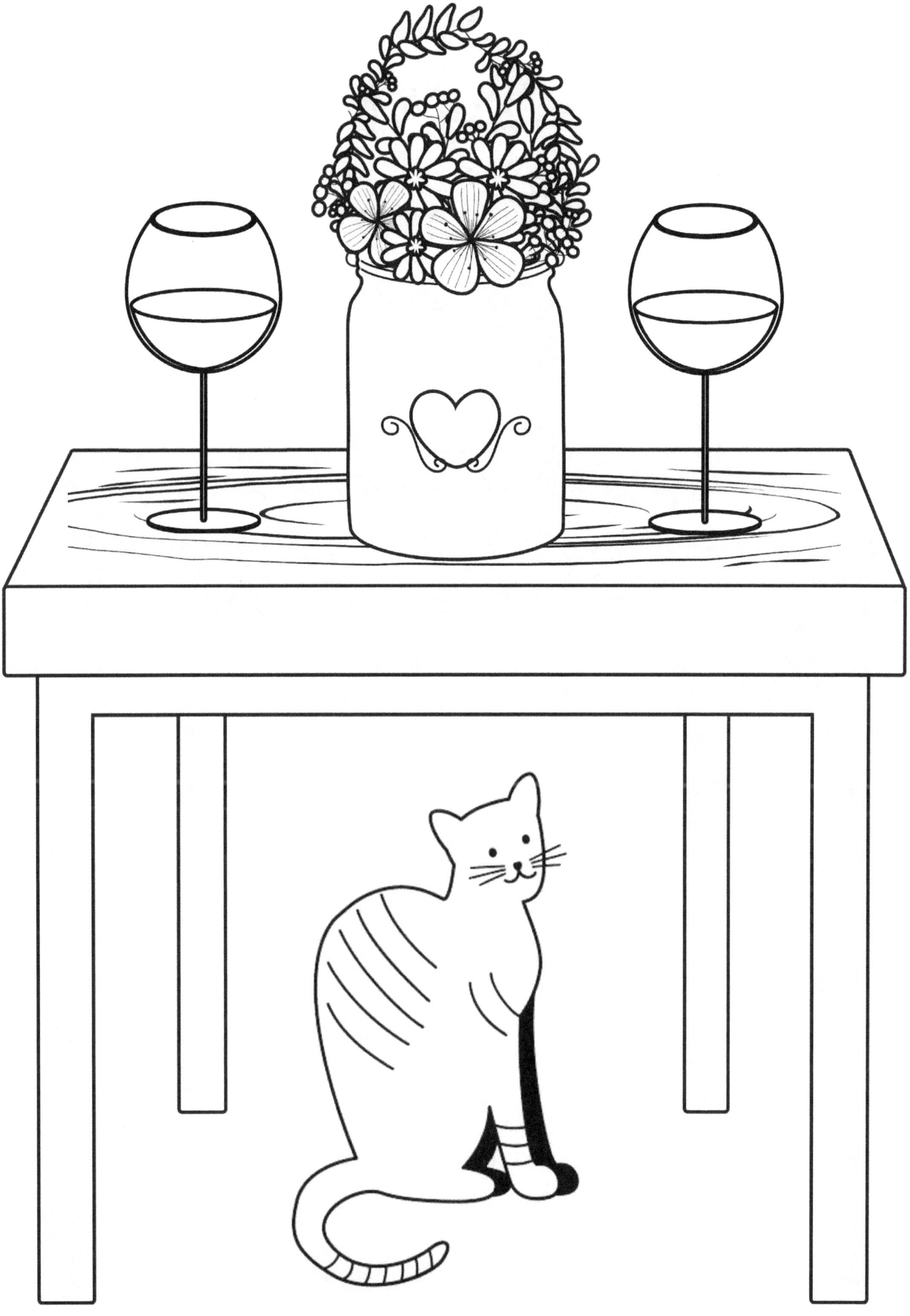

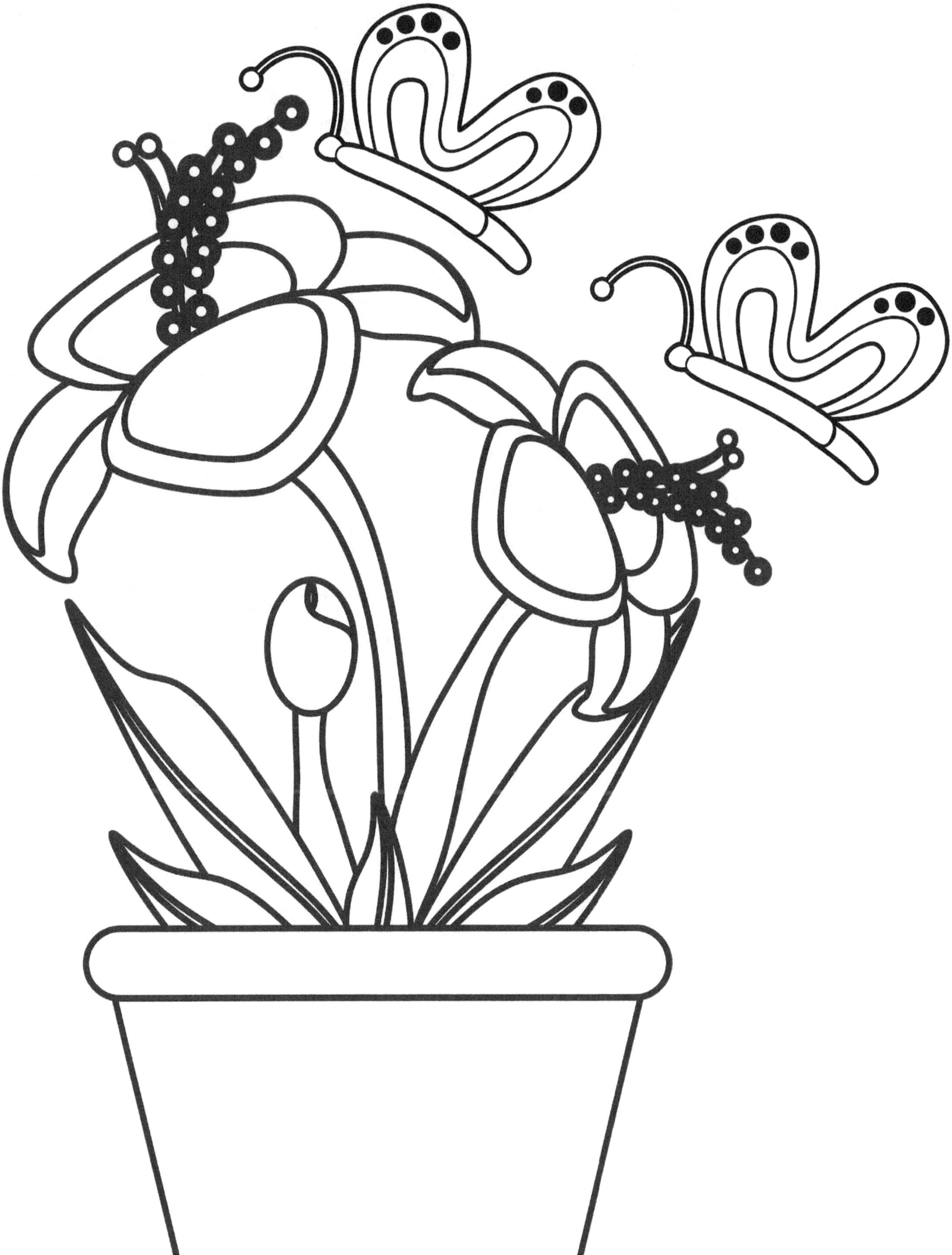

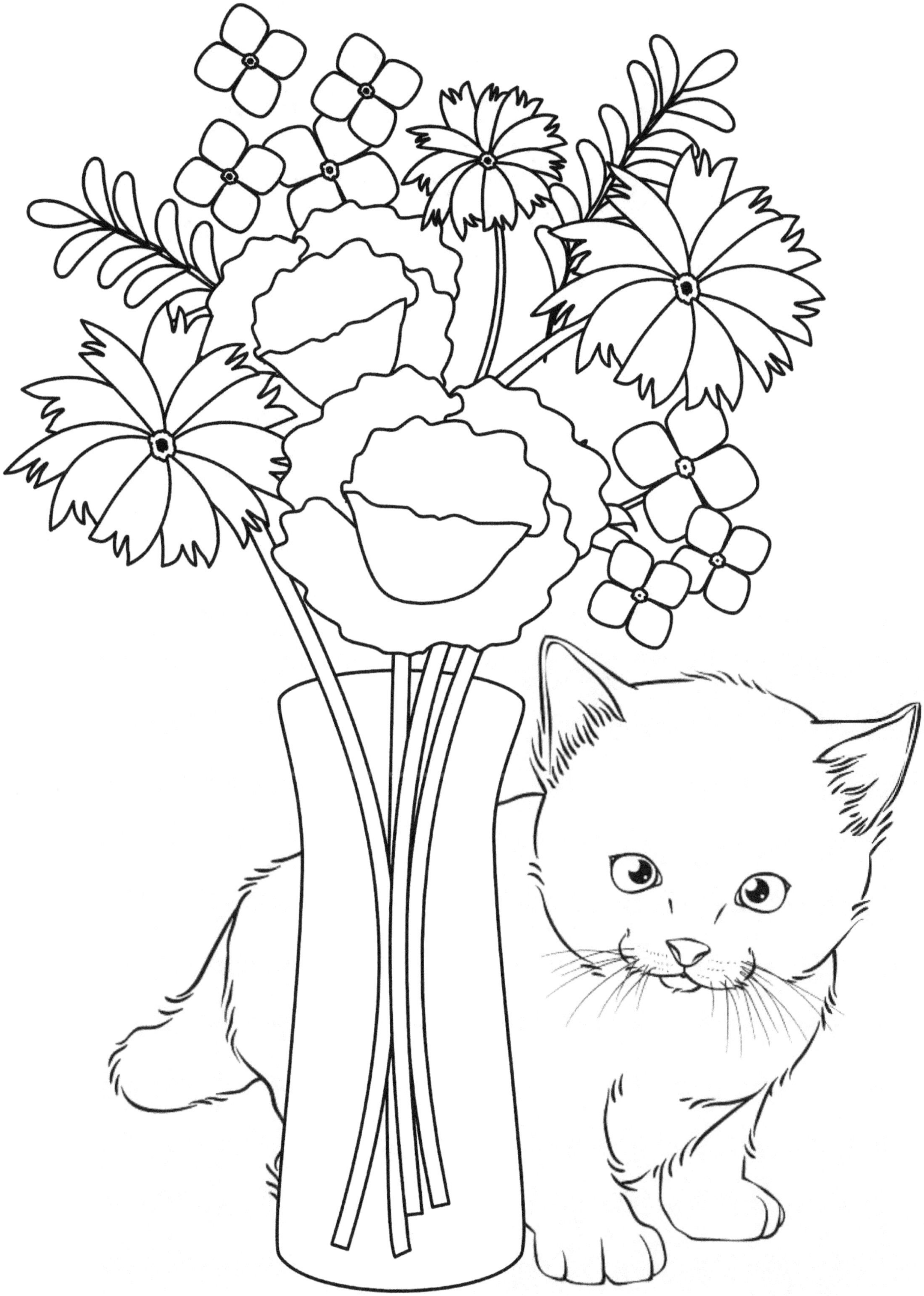

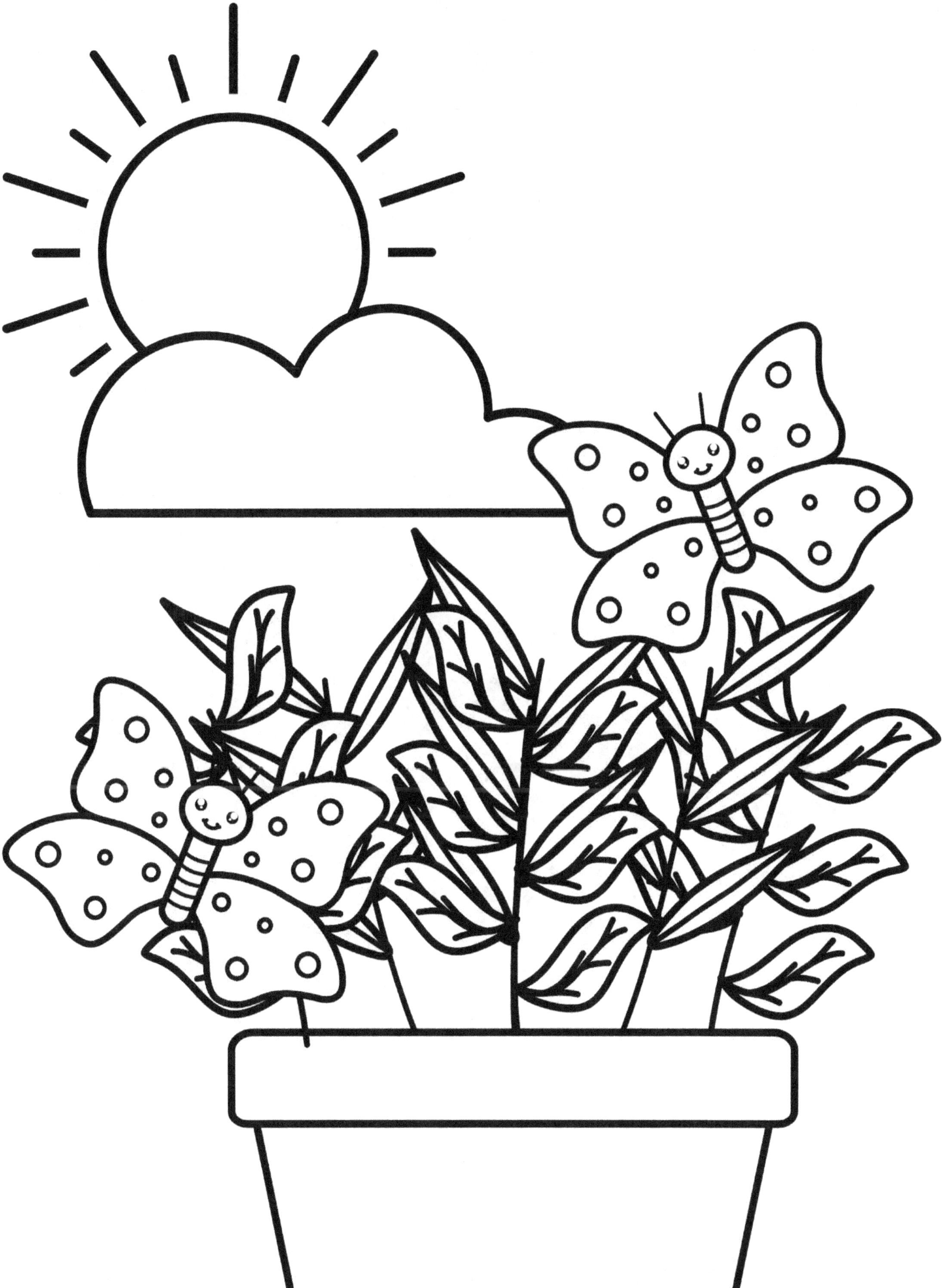

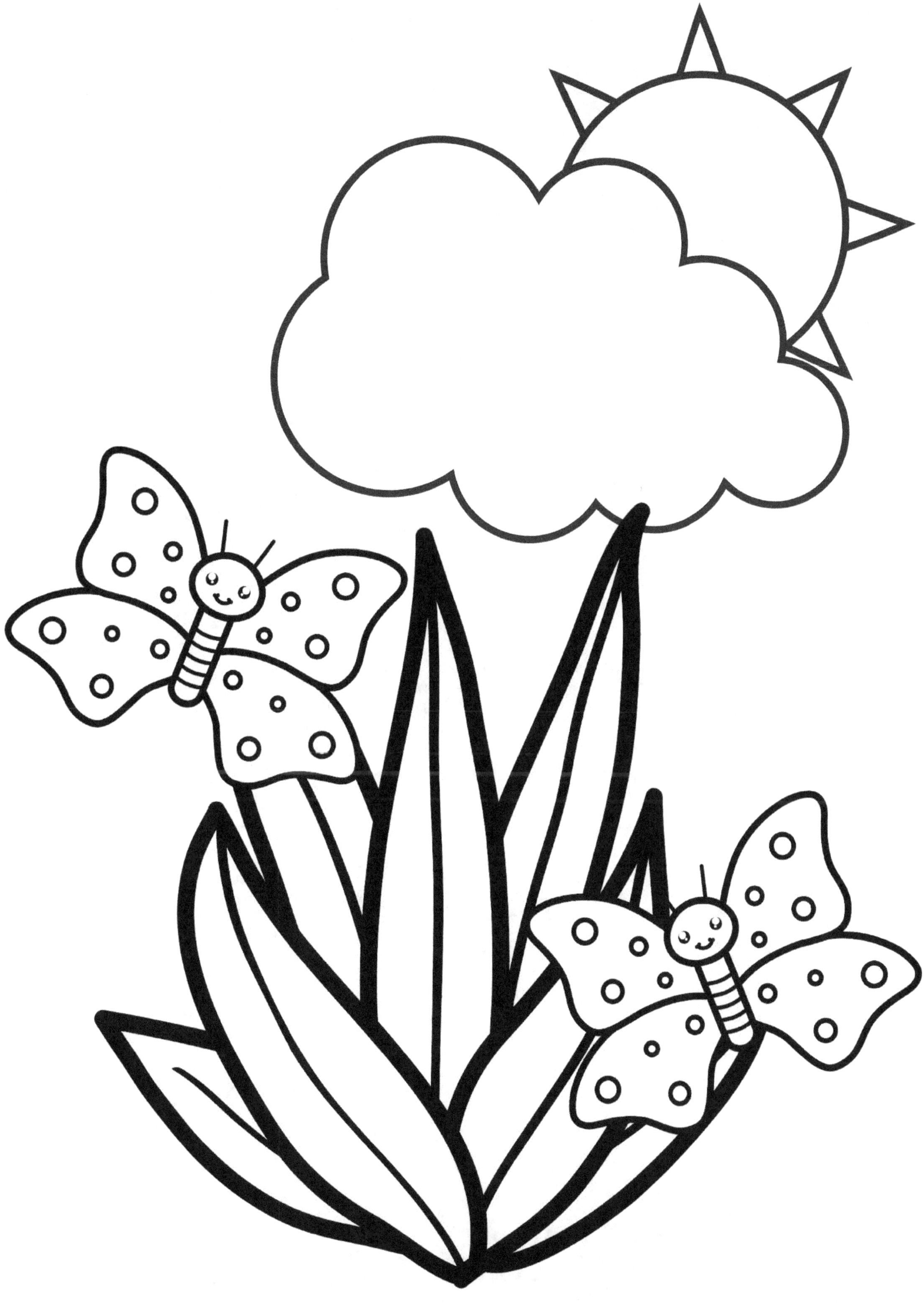

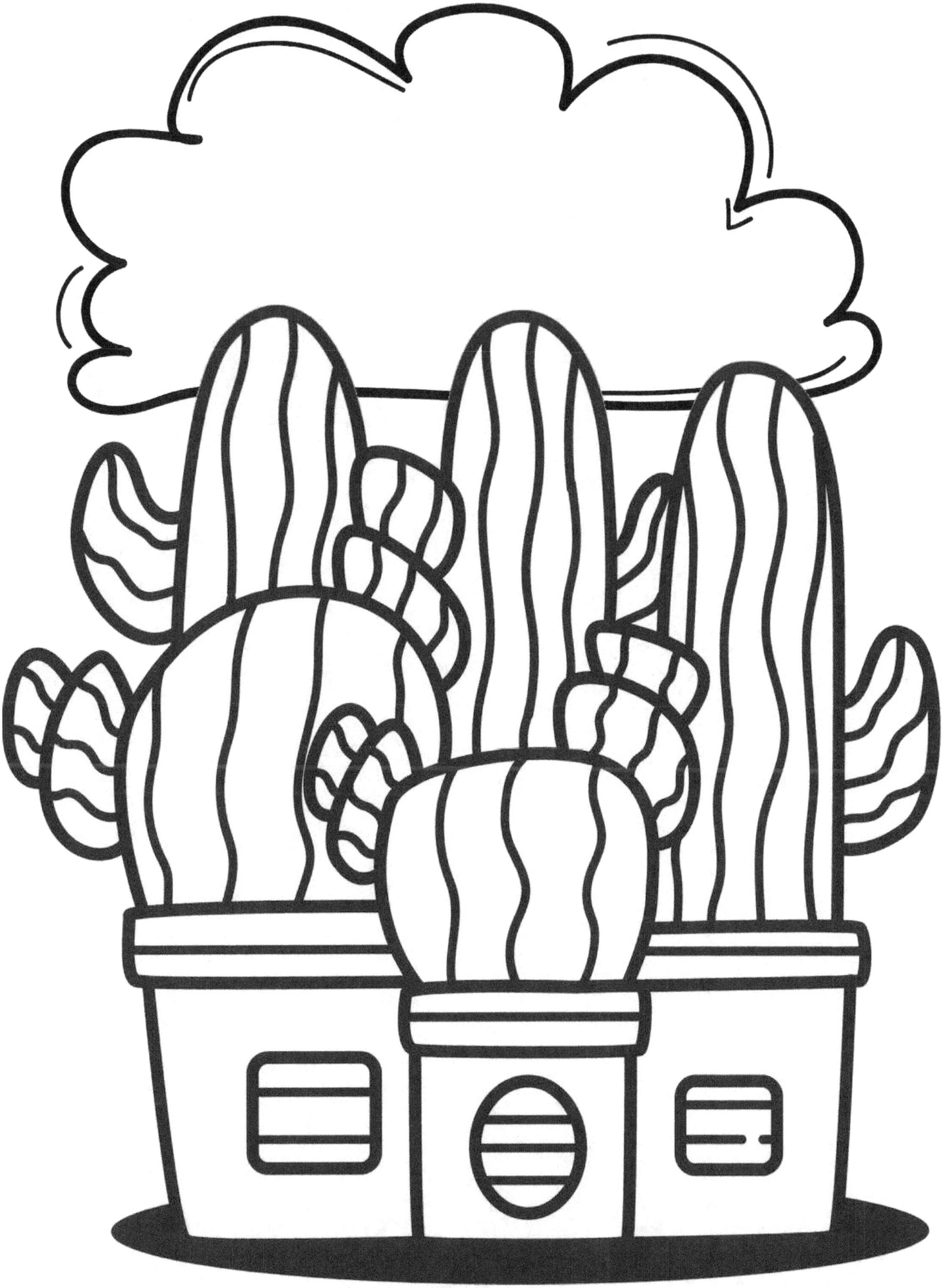

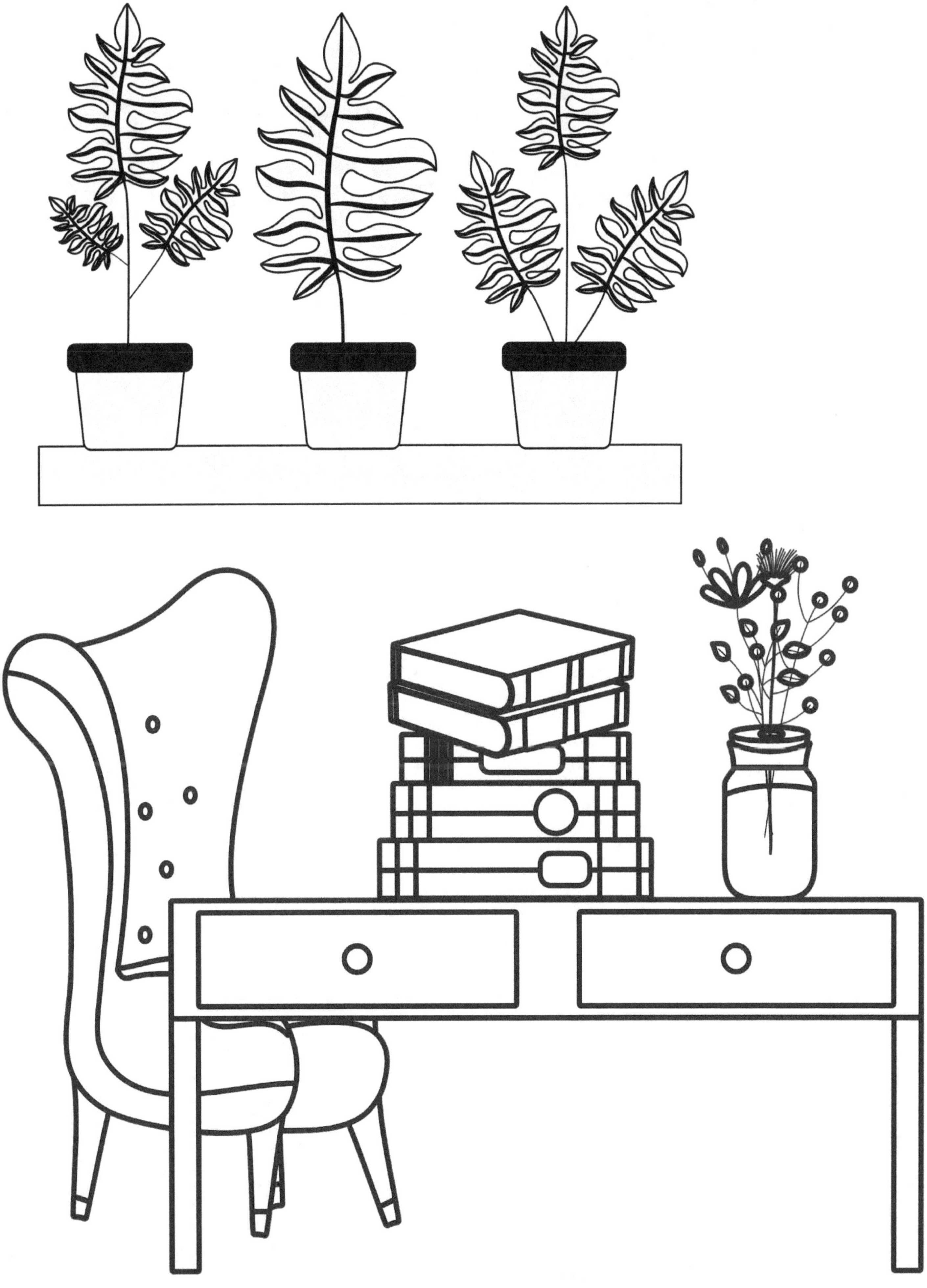

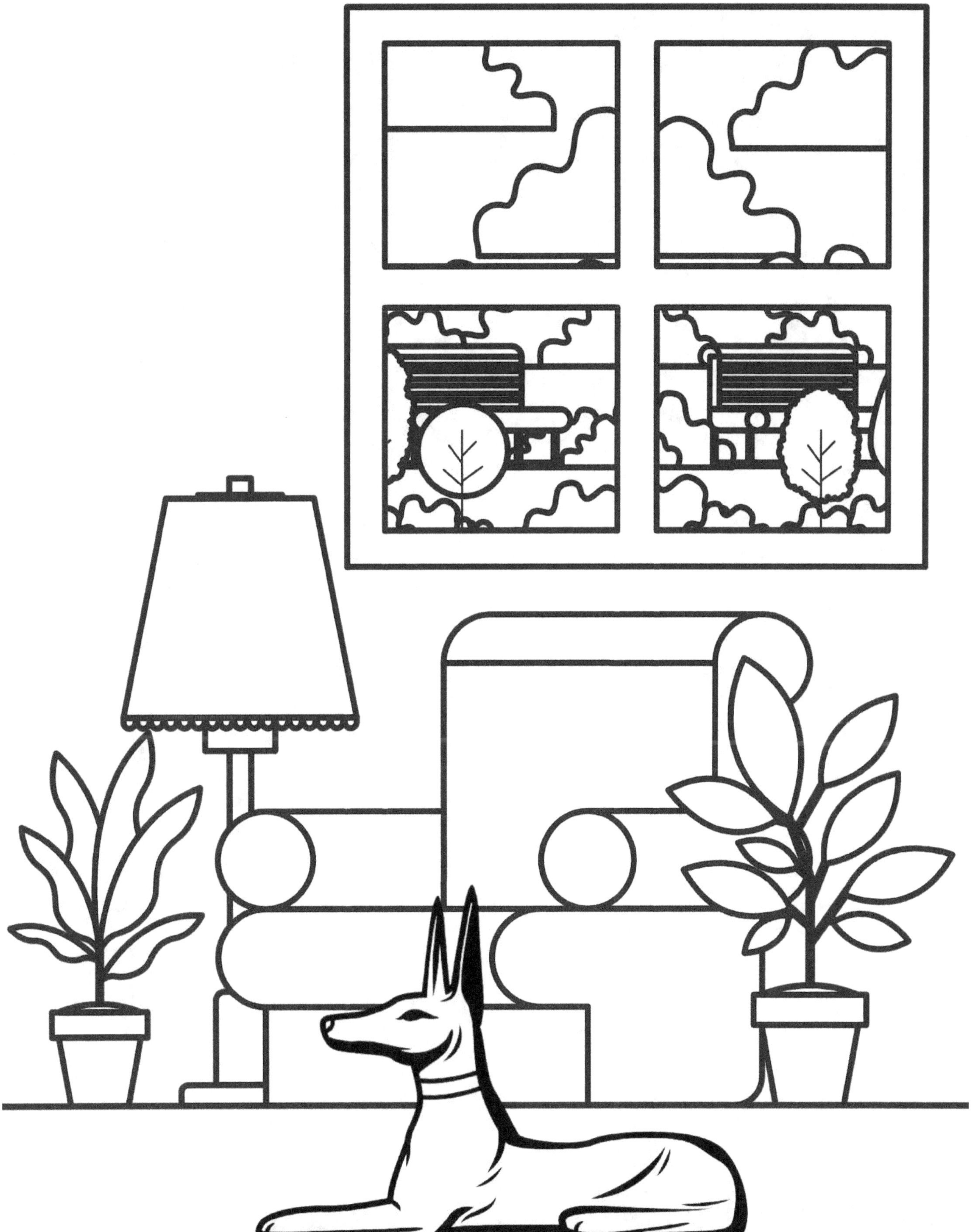

www.ingramcontent.com/pod-product-compliance
Lightning Source LLC
Chambersburg PA
CBHW080854220526
45467CB00008B/2503
* 9 7 9 8 6 9 1 9 3 6 7 6 0 *